"I CALL MY PEOPLE TO COME UP HIGHER"

By Joyce D. McGuire

As she diligently listened to the Spirit of the Lord

ISBN 10#09889500-4-9
ISBN 13#978-0-9889500-4-7
Printed in the United States of America

PUBLISHER/DESIGNER: CrossSounds Ministries Media
Website: www.CrossSounds.org
Contact: Diane@crosssounds.org

Contact Joyce McGuire: Rock of Ages Outreach Ministry
P.O. Box 5791
Anderson, SC 29623
Email: roaoutreachmin@att.net

ACKNOWLEDGEMENTS:

To my deceased parents who helped mold and shape my life in many ways, *Neal and Nellie McGuire.* Especially my precious Mother who recently passed away, who was always such a Godly influence to me; and my *grandparents* already gone to be with the Lord.

To my two wonderful daughters, *Angela* and *Faith,* may you forever be blessed in the Lord. Also my two departed children into Heaven's gates, *Douglas* and *Jennifer.* To my sisters, *Cheryl* and *Beth* and to my brother *Bradley*; also my precious *grandchildren.*

This book would not have been finished without my very close friends and *Pastors, Michel and Diane Bernardin.* Thank you both for your close walk with God and your influence on me and so many. A very special thank you for all the help in this book, especially to *Diane,* who agreed to work with me on getting it ready for publication.

My *spiritual Fathers* in the Lord and Pastors, who have imparted so very much into me were *Joe Parsons* in my early years and *James McCall,* now both deceased. Their wives meant much to me also. *Mrs. Parsons* and *Mildred McCall* is with the Lord now.

A very 'special acknowledgement' goes here to *Prophet Ray Witherington.* He was my Pastor and mentor for nearly 16 years, and *Linda Witherington,* his precious wife. Even though we are near the same age, Bro Ray has been a spiritual Father and constant encouragement in the faith to me. My two spiritual Mothers in the Lord, deceased were *Mildred Bennett* and *Mildred McCall*. What Godly life lessons and teachings, as I sat at their feet raising my children. I thank God for them.

Friends are so very important but at the risk of leaving someone out, I would like to just acknowledge my established 'prayer partners'- *Ella Merriwether, Diane Bernardin* and *Ann McMahan*. When you have someone to stand with you to pray, that is the greatest gift someone could ever give you, and you them.

DEDICATION

There is no doubt at all, that this book could *only* be dedicated to my Lord and Savior Jesus Christ, the Name above all names.

In a little Sunday School room at 8 years old, I asked Jesus in my heart, and He saved my soul. Never have I been sorry for that choice, only that I didn't always follow Him closer.

He is most worthy of *All* our praise and honor. Through many trials, faults and shortcomings, I have come. Still even so, the Lord has never even one time failed me. He is our very source of breath and life!

He is so wonderful, and matchless. Thank you God, for all your blessings and your sweet Holy Spirit which abides with us.

 I give You the Highest Praise!

RESOURCES

*ALL SCRIPTURE TAKEN FROM THE KING
JAMES VERSION BIBLE

THOMAS NELSON PUBLISHER

FORWARD

It is my wish here to explain, that you need to always *'try the spirits'* as you read the Prophetic utterances. We must always, at all times, do that with *anyone,* especially in this day and age. There is much deception out there and it is my desire to only print truth as I heard straight from the Spirit of God.

I can promise with all my heart, that I have sought much on these words. It was to make sure no error or flesh slipped in. My desire was to sit at the Lord's feet and hear His Words clearly. When we are sincere we want the people to only see His *'signature'* on anything spoken.

He still speaks today as yesterday. Many tears and weeping has gone into this. Much sorrow and pain is coming on this Nation and we must prepare. To listen close to the Father's heart beat is what I desire, and to do His blessed will.

May we draw closer and closer to Him. To any unsaved person who is reading, my prayer is to come to Jesus, while He is still calling.

ABOUT THE AUTHOR

Joyce McGuire has lived mainly in Anderson, S.C. most of her life. In the early 80's she lived in Belton, S.C. for nine years, seeking to grow in the Lord. During that time period she received the gift of the Holy Spirit. She has four children. Two of which have already passed to glory.

Most of her life she has been in Church, and worked however she was needed. In her early years from 10-18 years old, she traveled across 4 states singing with her youth choir from her church. At different times she has been a song leader, Sunday School teacher and a minister of helps. She was licensed and ordained to preach the gospel in 2004.

Her calling since 2006 has been as a 'Jail and Prison Evangelist'. Her heart's desire is to help those on the inside. She is now ordained through her Pastors at *CrossSounds Ministries* as a Chaplain, and is taking accredited courses through a College/Seminary. She has only gone into jails at this point to minister, with a lot of corresponding with inmates. Still, she feels the Lord is leading her into the Prisons soon to minister.

She has spoken and worked in various places in ministry. Among them are South Carolina, Alabama, New York and Ga. Through the years, she has been a 'prayer intercessor' in services. She now helps as an intercessor in the church she is attending, with her Pastors Michel and Diane Bernardin. Her heart is just to go or do wherever the Lord leads, and to be obedient in His service.

Contact Joyce: roaoutreachmin@att.net

7-19-2012 "A HOLY VISITATION IS UPON YOU"

"Thus saith the Lord: "In the stillness of the night have I called many of you, time and time again. Out of the darkness and into My marvelous light are you now walking. You are My children, called for such an hour as this. Many of you have been through the fire and the flames have not devoured you. In small or great matters do you obey Me. The tried and the true hear My voice and rise to the occasion. Into the fullness many of you have now come, and you are beginning to feel an anointing upon you that is stronger than ever before. Not many days hence will you walk in new power and see My hands perform many miracles. Do you not know yet children; I use you in My kingdom to establish righteousness?

You walk where I say walk, speak only what I put in your mouth and do good deeds unto all. It is a simple path of freedom, I have you walk in. Keep yourselves pure and unspotted from the world. Be not bound up with man's rules and regulations, but walk in new life with Me. Worry not about your future, but know every step has been ordained by Me, your God.

Do you not know yet children that I am a tender Father, and I desire only good things for you all? In the event tragedy strikes your life, it is for the greater good, to develop you. Sin is in the world and the enemy is rampant through the land, but I use all things for good in My kingdom, for those who love Me and keep My commandments. I separate not from My word. *"If you wonder what is truth from fallacy, try the spirits. If it is not from Me, it will not ring true or line up with My holy word."*

I gave a book of instruction for you to go by, and never do I depart from it. I am a holy God and put My righteousness upon the ones who yield to Me. I paid the cost at Calvary and declare every drop of blood that I shed was for your sins. Still many reject Me and put Me to an open shame. Was my sacrifice not enough? Would they have Me crucified again? They think not, but every time they deny Me they are saying My blood was not enough to clean them up. *"They go about trying to establish their own righteousness. It becomes self-righteousness, which is as filthy rags."* Many are so bound up; they go about with a religious spirit and seek to make others bound by their religious notions and ideas. People, when will you learn of my ways? I am a gentle Father and long to walk and talk with you daily. Many do know me in this personal way, but some of you never gave Me your whole heart. *"I desire to meet you in My secret hiding place. You will never be the same."* What I ask of you is to yield all of your heart, soul, mind and strength and quit trying to figure out life. I have it all already worked out, My children. Many shall be visited not many days hence, by angels. Some already have experienced their visitations.

Why do you hesitate My children, to know Me in the fullness? There is a holy hush coming on the land and many are feeling My presence in a new exciting way. The lame walk, the blind eyes see, the deaf hear and the dumb talk. You foolish who think it was for all back then, open your eyes and see what is going on around you. A spiritual awakening is upon you. Do you want to be a part? Get on fire and deny Me not, for I am pouring out My Spirit upon those who will let Me. You have kingdom authority, and you don't have to be afraid of anyone. You just have to get in alignment with My word and doubt not. Fare you well, My children. I send this love letter to you this night, to refresh and restore you, for many are weary and heavy hearted. I am coming back soon and am here now for those who recognize Me. My Spirit is falling across the land. Holy fire is upon you. This day is like none other and great miracles are happening.

"Cancers are being healed and nothing is impossible for those who believe." You see My children, I have always done the miraculous. You just need to believe. You are My instruments, My hands, and you shall even raise the dead. All things are possible. Let nothing stand in your way, and fight on the battlefield with victory in your souls."

12-13-12 "A Mean Bag Of Tricks And More."

The Spirit of the Lord speaks: "This is not for all. Surely not for the weak at heart, as some will not receive. Beware My children, for Santa Claus is toting a mean bag of tricks behind his back. He is mean and ugly and wears a disguise. What is his real name? Surely not ho, ho, ho. He is confusion, chaos, and trouble to many. He promises to deliver many times, but yet has not your address right for your little ones. ***Sometimes he only leaves you and them a lump of coal. Beware of him, the false God.***" Moving on: mistletoe, holly and such. You can't straddle the fence you say, and surely you can't, but yet I will reveal. Why is Christmas different than Halloween? Halloween is ***evil,*** a day of celebration of witches and the dark side. If you are truly celebrating My birth, there is a difference. I know the heart. The tree decorated up, is a sight to behold, is it not? Does it bring you joy? Does it bring you pleasure? Yes, for I will even use it. Why does man take the scripture in the old and put bondage on you? I will reveal. What do I say about the Christmas tree and celebrating this time of year? Many will tell you do it not, and even give you the scriptures out of the Old Testament. Write it down child.

Jer. 10:1 "Hear ye the word which the Lord speaketh unto you, o house of Israel:

2 thus saith the Lord, learn not the way of the heathen, and be not dismayed at the signs of heaven; for the heathen are dismayed at them.

3 for the customs of the people are vain: for one cutteth a tree out of the forest, the work of the hands of the workman, with the axe.

4 they deck it with silver and with gold; they fasten it with nails and with hammers, that it move not.

5 they are upright as the palm tree, but speak not: they must needs be borne, because they cannot go. Be not afraid of them; for they cannot do evil, neither also is it in them to do good....

9 silver spread into plates is brought from tarshish, and gold

from Uphaz, the work of the workman, and of the hands of the founder: blue and purple is their clothing: they are all the work of cunning men.
10 but the Lord is the true God, He is the living God, and an everlasting King: at His wrath the earth shall tremble, and the nations shall not be able to abide His indignation.
What does verse three here mean, daughter? Many will not understand and get angry even at you, for bringing this forward, but I have them to take it up with Me. Tell them all to try the spirits and see if this is My hand that doth truly write this? It is a spiritual meaning. It is **works** I am talking about. In verse four you will see that the decorations have begun, glorifying self I say. I give illustrations all through My word.

Apply them wisely, children. Are you heathen or Spirit filled believers, I say unto you? Are you sitting at My feet, worshiping Me? Could these verses have been misapplied by well-meaning saints of God? For surely I say unto you, many of them love Me and try to please only Me, but I will reveal further. Love Me, not the rule book. I will show you when you are in error surely. Now look at verse nine above. Seek a spiritual meaning always first, My children. *"It is not the modern day Christmas tree I warn you about, but lusting after the world. The works of men's hands is the issue!"*

Never confuse it with faith and works operating together I say. Joy is in the hearts of the people a little more at this time of year. What causes it? The reflections of Christmas past, but only in part. Some have only sad bitter memories, this time of year. It is just a time when you feel more love in the air. Whenever you celebrate My birth, then celebrate it. Might it be also in another month? Be fully persuaded in your own mind I say unto you.Be not caught up in bondage either way. Straight narrow paths for your feet, My little ones. Now I will answer a question that I ask you. Am I pleased with all the commercialism going on this time of year? You say yes, guess again. **Man goes too far.** Keep it simple, all things. Keep it simple little ones; I speak unto your heart again. **Celebrate life** I say unto you. The greatest gift ever been given is Me. I poured out My life unto you on the rugged cross. Great pain did I suffer for your sins. I was born to die, to live again, and I live forevermore. Again I say just celebrate life. Celebrate Me. I will be pleased and that is thus saith the Lord."

4-12-13 "A New Song Or An Old"

The Spirit of the Lord spoke: "Gone are the days of wine and roses for many, yet here are the days of wine and roses for some. What do I mean children? I speak it before. You must not ever lose your focus, and that I do ever warn and mean. Sure have a sweet love song in your hearts, for many have been hurt and wounded bad, and the cost was great. Still, when I put a great love in your heart, it shall be right. The God of heaven never speaks division, but unity. To ye of little faith, now do I speak: why do you not move on, when I speak?

You align yourselves with wrong characters, ones of a single purpose to work evil and wreak havoc in My blessed kingdom. Get off the totem pole and the dance, I do speak unto you. How do you know if this is for you, my children? If it pricks your heart, it surely is. You see My children; I bring My beloved ones warnings. *"A sweet love song"* you must have, but not in the enemies camp. For surely I say on: if you dance to the tune of the pied piper, you shall surely come up lacking. *"The song starts out sweet but comes out sour and bitter in the end."*
Repent and turn around chosen ones, I do say unto your hearts. I will be your sweet love song and ever move in that department for a husband, wife or mate for you, if you so desire. *"Only let Me put it together, at the right time."*

Did you not know My children and My beloved ones, I am sweeter than the sweetest honeycomb you may taste on your lips? Go in My service and do My blessed will and I will order and direct your steps. I have spoken and that is thus saith the Lord your God, this day."

10-7-2012 "A Strong Warning To All"

"The Lord does speak through this servant this day. Let all be consumed upon the altar of sacrifice. Remove the petty differences, and rise up and be counted in My kingdom. Many of you are too readily offended, and I'll have it not. Time is short and soon to be done away with. March on, but be prepared for greater battles. I am fine tuning many of you, sharpening you, I might say. Battle weary are you, but sometimes it is your own fault. I do not have you to fight in every battle. Some are of your own choosing. What do I mean? You get weary and wore down, but a lot of times, you are choosing wrong. You enter into debates which I have you not. Strife, murmurings and complaining are not of Me.

Surely I say on: when you enter into controversy with another, the devil is winning. I have you to lay down the strife and contention, and be on the winning side. Quit trading camps, I say. I speak a sharp word, My children. You weary Me with all your going back and forth. You are Mine, so be still and hear the sound of My voice. I speak further this day: be at peace and quit judging your brothers and sisters. Many of you are fighting one another. I will deal with the heart. Take your hands and mouth off people, unless I speak to deliver a word. A cutting tongue can destroy much, and wound a spirit mightily.

If the Lord's camp is divided, you won't win I say. Quit changing sides, as the confusion will only get greater. Grow up I say, get off the milk bottle, and take on some meat. There are little ones I have you to protect and nurture, and you are getting too 'sidetracked.' Still many, this is not to personally.

They are strong in Me, and obey the sound of My voice. *"You will know, if it is for you."* Yet I speak on My children: none of you have arrived yet. I tell you this before and I do tell you again. This sister is fearing Me as she writes this. I always have you to do an examination and check your own heart, no matter who you are.

Many mighty in Me have fallen I say. The lust of a man or woman has brought many to a piece of bread. Also, many more temptations can beset you. Watch and pray, and stay meek. ***"Know it is by My grace and mercy you stand at all."*** It is time for harvest, that is why the fight has gotten greater. The enemy has set traps for you, in many directions. It is a time like no other. Heed the sound of My voice and live. Again, I say, ***prepare*** for greater battle. Keep your hearts pure. Love you every one I do, but I am preparing you I say. Know evil is in the world. Many of you are My chosen elect and the outpouring that is about to come on the world before My millennium reign, is phenomenal. ***"Still you must know the ones in darkness will be even more terrifying and satan is out to frighten you. My saints in these end times will not fear anyone or anything!"***

You will rise up with victory in your souls, and defeat the enemy in the land. Just know, you should love the people and hate the evil spirits terrifying them. Never give place to demons. Rebuke them when I tell you. ***"Speak the word and never argue with spirits from hell."*** You can only go so far with a person not wanting complete deliverance. When I tell you to move back, it is in your best interest to do it. The Spirit of the Lord will always lead you. Just obey Me quickly, or you will be consumed. A breath of fresh air, I am breathing on you My children and My saints. I rebuke those I love and chasten them. I have you not to get heady or high minded. Again I love you, and walk beside you always. I am a God that will perform all I have promised unto you. Be encouraged this day, My children."

3-19-2013 "A Sweet Love Song"

Hearing from the Lord: "It is a time like never before child, daughter. Gone are the days of wine and roses I say before and I say again. **"Yet I say on: *"It is still all about commitment and focus; I do speak unto your hearts."*** In the beginning of time, I put man with woman and woman with man for a purpose. It was a holy purpose, one of My design. It was truly so mankind would not be lonely, did I put a woman with him. She was to walk right beside, in step and beat with him, every beat of his heart, I do say and speak. What did I say in My word? She was created as a help meet. Let's explore: When two like minds and hearts draw near and join, a lot is accomplished in My kingdom. I speak further that the marriage bed is still undefiled, only whoremongers and adulterers I will judge. Proof is in the pudding I speak. When two hearts of like minds and like visions join I speak again, much is accomplished in My kingdom. Two shall be as one and become one. Draw nigh, hear the sound of My voice and live. Many have thrown loves song away in the past. It was too hard for you.

Surely your heart had been rended too bad. Even I say bitterness tried to creep in. Now I speak on: Time for a new day, a new song My beloved ones. Caution I have had you to use. Still I say, many of you have not used wisdom, and stayed too long with your beloveds and your heart was hurt. *"When I tell you to break from a person, it is time. You women and you men, when you consider a mate, you need to line up everything with My word, for I never put together a couple who do not spiritually agree."* What else do I join a woman and a man for? I re-create life through a woman's womb. When a man plants his seed in her, an offspring occurs; a precious life I do say unto your hearts. A next new generation begins. It is of me. It has always been of me, but yet many have chosen wrong and much sorrow occurred. Holy children from a holy connection; one generation to the other; teaching My commandments, My statues and walking therein, are what I ordain.
I speak further: seek not a wife or a husband for that is where you lack understanding. Be whole complete in Me and I will join you with My intended, if it is to be. What do I mean children, little ones?
I know your hearts that you desire someone to walk with, but yet I say on: let Me do the choosing for I know best. Just let Me lead and put them before you and join two hearts, I say. What happens is you try to figure it out many times, and you never can. Then you take steps to find your beloved, and that is where you do err. Now I speak the conclusion of the matter. Many desire not a mate and I truly honor that. You shall be as a eunuch

before Me, and much good will be accomplished in My kingdom. Holy, sold out to Me and seeking My face. Let one not judge the other. Only I speak a final word of warning: those that have a wife, be as those that have not. Also I will say, ye women the same. Put Me first in your marriages and then the other next. Then it will all come out right, and that is thus saith the Lord your God."

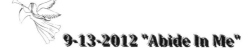

9-13-2012 "Abide In Me"

The Lord speaks: "I would have you to know the sound of My voice. Know ye not trouble is surely in the land? I will reveal and show mysteries to who will open their understanding. The mark of the beast is at hand, and as I tell you before I tell you again, *"take My mark instead".* The empire of satan is coming down. I reveal truth. Revel in it, and not the lie. Satan has the world deceived. The false system is coming down. Babylon has fallen and is ruling and reigning no more in the hearts of My chosen elect. What that is about? You wear My mark well, 777 ye ones who have spiritual understanding.

Get in the overflow and take your brothers and sisters higher with you. I speak words of peace unto you. *"The rider on the pale horse speaks death and deception. Did you not know death is the deception?"* Did I not say in My word, ye shall never die but live eternally? To leave this earth in death, as you know it, is to be instantly with Me. Know ye not I conquered death, hell and the grave, when I gave My life's blood for you, My children on the bloody cross? *"I had the keys with Me, when I rose again and came up out of the grave".* The grave cloth could never hold Me. When you belong unto Me, you shall never die but move into eternity, in another realm. I speak on: *faith is the key.* Never give up, and abide in Me always. Love you I do. Persevere."

12-18-12 "Admonitions To My Daughters And Sons"

Hearing the Lord speak: "Some that even call themselves by My name, want more. What do they want more of? *"They want more power and control over people and situations."* I have it not so. They talk a pretty talk; they walk a pretty straight line or do they? They be in err, and once it is opened up, you will see. Buyer beware, I say unto your hearts. Many women have yielded to the smooth talking man. He wants to control, I say unto you. It is surely a downfall of women.

They want the love, the romance and they often give their hearts, inadvisably so, at times. Gird on new strength, you women of God. For I will reveal much more. The pain, the sorrow in your heart, I have seen my daughters. Many are bruised or broken, but surely I am sewing you up. It is a quick work I will do, for I need you in the fields working for me. Many of the men failed to see your great beauty daughters, and they desired another and another. I am visiting them for their sin.

"You have allowed too much control and I say take it back now." Harlot system is working, even in many of the ones I have called. You need to see this. Love Me tender, love Me true, and then they truly just move on to another. They cast you under their feet and stomp on you. Move on I say unto you daughter, woman of God. Take on the blood-stained banner and arise, for I have new work for you. Many in these last days will surely be laid on a shelf. They will not repent and keep going in the same old paths. New work I have for them, but yet they do not get all things right with Me. *"Man or woman must yield all the way to the foot of the cross."* Do you want the shelf and to be laid on it like an old discarded rag doll, no good for anything or anyone? Make up your mind quickly, for I am playing no more. There was surely a time I winked at sin, but no longer. Now we go on to you men, and what happens with some of you. You yield to the *Jezebel spirit,* and it rends you. The woman not sold out to God, with a controlling spirit, will rip you apart every time. Have her not, as she controls and she wounds with a passion. Feel not

sorry for her. She has brought many a man to a piece of bread. Be strong you men, and quit giving place to the beauty in her. There is a worldly beauty, without the quiet adornment of heart, and it is trash and rubbish I do say. A true woman of God has a meek spirit and a quiet spirit. Does that mean she has nothing to say? No it means, she is not loud and stubborn. ***"The witchcraft spirit is so! It is an alluring spirit, set on fire from the pits of hell."*** Make up your minds you daughters and you sons. It is all about coming closer unto Me. See these great truths, for I will strengthen you and cause you to stand My little ones. Hearts on fire, be on fire for Me. Come sup with Me and at My feet humbly bow. I have spoken and love you I surely do.

11-28-2013 "America Can Rise Again; Out Of The Ashes, Up To The People."

Word of the Lord: "Have I not spoken My child, that I am bringing this country down unto your heart? My wrath is upon her but still I always leave people with a hope. Who can hear My voice? What does it say in My word? Find it and post it daughter. I never go or come apart from My word. **2 Chronicles 7:14** "If My people, which are called by My name, shall humble themselves, and pray, and seek My face, and turn from their wicked ways; then will I hear from heaven, and will forgive their sin, and will heal their land. What is happening? ***"The remnant is being saved; the remnant is being renewed."*** Mercy is being shown on my people even from every land, America included. Do you call yourselves by My name? Are you spiritual Israel or not My people? Did you not know I call a holy people unto Myself to behold My face and worship Me in truth and in spirit, My children? I love you sons and daughters of Zion. In the midst of utter destruction, even I am! When you hear My voice speak unto you, yield *quickly* and you will get through all things. Even in the midst of persecution and destruction I walk and talk with my people. Do you love me? Then keep My commandments, plain and simple. If there is sin in the camp get rid of it before it destroys you. Surely, I am calling you to a new walk and a new talk in Me, My beloved. Deeper than you have ever been do I call you to go with Me. Go behind the curtain, the veil, the most holy of holies with Me your Adonai, your king. Intimacy level, am I calling My beloved to walk in. It is to a new height and new depth I am bringing you into, My people who hear My voice. Come alive, read My word and partake of it fully. Only I warn you My children, rightly divide it.

Much discernment is needed. Did you not know I will bestow and give good gifts to all who hunger and thirst after righteousness? Desire the sincere milk of the word that you may grow thereby. Count the stars in heaven! You can't? Then why do you think you can figure things out? I surely know the stars by name; the planet; the galaxy. I Am that I Am and I created all things into existence by My word. I spoke it into existence. I am coming back soon for a people prepared as a bride for her husband. I Am that I Am and surely I am refreshing My people who will listen and hearken unto Me. Who is I Am? The God who gives you your very next breath is who. Worship Me, My children in spirit and in truth and your days will be richer and fuller and with no discrepancy and no lack. My mark is upon you and many of you do I speak this day. Get rid of the hindrances, for to a new place I desire and long to take you, I surely do speak again and that is thus saith the Lord thy God this day."

3-18-2014 "Are You Ready?"

"War is coming to the land. It is soon and it is now. Rise up My people in My authority and put or place on the whole armor of God. End time army is marching forward. Revival fires are spreading, the same time great destruction is occurring. The Babylonian system is coming down. I am revealing much of what is coming on the land. Approved unto Me you must be. Walk in My anointing, My power, My beloved people. Nothing is as it appears at times. Hidden talks, hidden agendas are taking place behind closed doors. All things are not well in the government, yet I speak a word of hope to My people. Know My voice and heed My warnings, My children. Lay all things on an altar of sacrifice. ***"Sweeping revival is in the land and is occurring in spots, but much error is trying to slip in, My beloved ones and I will expose it."*** Whenever you hear My name mentioned, am I being glorified or are the works of men's hands? You will know the difference. Do nothing without a cost. Pay the price to walk in My fullness. Great trials are ahead but yet great victory. I will see you through all things. I alone will succor you and lift your hands in battle. This new army is rising up with new courage and new valor. As in the book of **Joel 2nd Chapter** you shall see and you shall know.

Joel 2:1 "Blow ye the trumpet in Zion, and sound an alarm in My holy mountain: let all the inhabitants of the land tremble: for the day of the Lord cometh, for it is nigh at hand;

2 a day of darkness and of gloominess, a day of clouds and of thick darkness, as the morning spread upon the mountains: a great people and a strong; there hath not been ever the like, neither shall be any more after it, even to the years of many generations.

3 a fire devoureth before them; and behind them a flame burneth: the land is as the Garden of Eden before them, and behind them a desolate wilderness; yea, and nothing shall escape them.

4 the appearance of them is as the appearance of horses; and as horsemen, so shall they run.

5 like the noise of chariots on the tops of mountains shall they leap, like the noise of a flame of fire that devoureth the stubble, as a strong people set in battle array.

6 before their face the people shall be much pained: all faces shall gather blackness.

7 they shall run like mighty men; they shall climb the wall like men of war; and they shall march every one on his ways, and they shall not break their ranks:

8 neither shall one thrust another; they shall walk every one in his path: and when they fall upon the sword, they shall not be wounded.

9 they shall run to and fro in the city; they shall run upon the wall, they shall climb up upon the houses; they shall enter in at the windows like a thief.

10 the earth shall quake before them; the heavens shall tremble: the sun and the moon shall be dark, and the stars shall withdraw their shining:

11 and the Lord shall utter His voice before His army: for His camp is very great: for He is strong that executeth His word: for the day of the Lord is great and very terrible; and who can abide it?

12 therefore also now, saith the Lord, turn ye even to Me with all your heart, and with fasting, and with weeping, and with mourning:

13 and rend your heart, and not your garments, and turn unto the Lord your God: for He is gracious and merciful, slow to anger, and of great kindness, and repenteth Him of the evil.

14 who knoweth if He will return and repent, and leave a blessing behind Him; even a meat offering and a drink offering unto the Lord your God?

15 blow the trumpet in Zion, sanctify a fast, call a solemn assembly:

16 gather the people, sanctify the congregation, assemble the elders, gather the children, and those that suck the breasts: let the bridegroom go forth of His chamber, and the bride out of her closet.

17 let the priests, the ministers of the Lord, weep between the porch and the altar, and let them say, spare thy people, O Lord, and give not thine heritage to reproach, that the heathen should rule over them: wherefore should they say among the people, where is their God?

18 then will the Lord be jealous for His land, and pity His people.

19 yea, the Lord will answer and say unto His people, behold, I will send you corn, and wine, and oil, and ye shall be satisfied therewith: and I will no more make you a reproach among the heathen:

20 but I will remove far off from you the northern army, and will drive him into a land barren and desolate, with his face toward the east sea, and his hinder part toward the utmost sea, and his stink shall come up, and his ill savour shall come up, because he hath done great things.

21 fear not, O land; be glad and rejoice: for the Lord will do great things.

22 be not afraid, ye beasts of the field: for the pastures of the wilderness do spring, for the tree beareth her fruit, the fig tree and the vine do yield their strength.

23 be glad then, ye children of Zion, and rejoice in the Lord your God: for He hath given you the former rain moderately, and He will cause to come down for you the rain, the former rain, and the latter rain in the first month.

24 and the floors shall be full of wheat, and the vats shall overflow with wine and oil.

25 and I will restore to you the years that the locust hath eaten, the cankerworm, and the caterpillar, and the palmerworm, My great army which I sent among you.

26 and ye shall eat in plenty, and be satisfied, and praise the name of the Lord your God, that hath dealt wondrously with you: and My people shall never be ashamed.

27 and ye shall know that I am in the midst of Israel and that I am the Lord your God, and none else: and My people shall never be ashamed.

28 and it shall come to pass afterward, that I will pour out My Spirit upon all flesh; and your sons and your daughters shall prophesy, your old men shall dream dreams, your young men shall see visions:

29 and also upon the servants and upon the handmaids in those days will I pour out My Spirit.

30 and I will shew wonders in the heavens and in the earth, blood, and fire, and pillars of smoke.

31 the sun shall be turned into darkness, and the moon into blood, before the great and terrible day of the Lord come.

32 and it shall come to pass, that whosoever shall call on the name of the Lord shall be delivered: for in Mount Zion and in Jerusalem shall be deliverance, as the Lord hath said, and in the remnant whom the Lord shall call."

Seek Me with all your heart, all your being. Come before My presence with singing as My holy word says. Anointing is upon you. To many of you this day, I am bringing you higher, higher in My courts. I say on: "Preach the word, be instant in season out of season. Let all things go but coming before My face. Let Me consume your being, come first in your heart and lives. Grow stronger in Me, My beloved children. I will lead and I will guide. My sheep know My voice and follow Me. My tenderness, My love, I pour out upon you this day and will not leave you in a blind spot but will see you through all things. Get on the bandwagon. I am leading and I am drawing you closer and that is thus saith the Lord your God this day."

8-23-2012 "Battleground Is Here"

Thus saith the Lord God: "Surely goodness and mercy has kept you all the days of your life. I will be merciful on who I will be merciful. I have you look straight ahead My children, for the battle is going to get rougher. What is ahead? Fierce winds are blowing. I speak on. Battle weary are many of you and good cause have you to be. Many do not know that you are being fought by the prince of the very power of the air. Look up, for your redemption surely draweth nigh. As I tell you before I am coming back after a spotless church. My bride is being arrayed in white linen and pure and spotless shall she be. Proof is in the pudding. Develop your talents now and use every ability I give you. All My children have gifts I have given them. I have you stir up the gifts that lieth in you. As I tell you before, visitations are all around. Believe it not?

My angels and My children who have translated or have passed from death to life are all around you. *"Wake up My people, wake up and again I say unto thee wake up."* You see, but you do not see. You think it is an isolated occurrence and I say no they are on every hand. They walk and talk among you. Sometimes they are seen and sometimes not. Many of you know whereas I speak. My beloved I have you not blinded any longer. Resist not ye chosen ones, for I will continue to reveal many things unto you through not only this sister, but many of My chosen ones. I am visiting with strange dreams and visions and you understand them not. Ye are supposed to be seeking Me on these and I will reveal. Write down from your remembrance and come unto Me and I will give you more understanding. Many in My body of believers do have interpretations as no one is a one man show. Work together always and seek Me. The church body should always be working in **one accord. "You will not withstand if you hear not the sound of My voice and obey Me."** My Holy Ghost power is being poured out across the land, but also My fury is being unleashed. This servant is crying out now so you will heed My warnings. Blow the trumpet and sound My alarm to all. Be watchmen on the wall and tarry not any longer. All across the United States and I say even the world, My judgement is being unleashed. Do you not care?

You say you do, but many of you still do not give Me all. **"Quit hanging out of the boat before it capsizes, I say unto you."** The wicked have to turn loose of their wealth for I have commanded it. It will be redistributed to My beloved children. I have My children to come alive and start putting to practice the things I speak unto your heart. Judgement I say again, has struck the nation. The reason I speak so sharply at times is I have you leading My people out. I am calling you to prepare as never before. Not so much stocking up in these troublesome, perilous times, but rending your heart unto Me.

Ye are a chosen vessel and I will use you when you get **awake** to deliver My people. You see My children it saddens me to bring destruction, but there is no other way. **"Many will cry back out unto Me and I have you tend to them."** Many camps will be set up for the wounded. Death will be everywhere, but I am strengthening My people who are chosen to go across the land and minister to people's needs. Never worry about how, only obey Me, for I will fill you with a joy that you thought not possible. Even in the midst of destruction, your joy shall be full and your peace many will wonder of. I am Jehovah-Jireh and I speak loud enough to be heard and clear enough to be understood. Feast at my table and drink from My well and ye shall never thirst again and that is thus saith the Lord your God. Prove me this day. My love and anointing is poured out unto you and I will perform My words unto you. You will never be the same. Love you My people, I do."

10-2-2012 "Be Faithful Till The End"

I hear the Lord speaking: "Children, this day I send you greetings and comfort. A special word here is needed, for many of you have been through the extreme heat of satan's fire lately. Did you not know My children it is for a reason? What I mean for you to get in your spirit this day, is there is a new day dawning. Just because you are in a 'transition period' does not mean there are not battles and warfare. Just remember I have overcome and so shall you. ***"You overcome by the blood of the lamb and the word of your testimony."*** Many of you have been tested almost beyond your endurance. There is a reason. Like the old saying if footmen tire you what will horses do?

I must bring you to and through these difficult places My children to prove you. Only My hand can spare you and protect you. Satan's devices are devious. Doubtful have been many of you that you would even make it through. The fire and tribulation has gotten so much stronger, that you would drown if I did not intervene. Satan can go no further than I allow. He tells a lie and many believe it. Stop yielding to his ugly punishment. The joy of the lord is surely your strength. I must prepare you for the days ahead, so think it not strange of all that is coming against you. You my people are coming into a new day. A day of atonement is upon you. I have redeemed mankind unto Myself. The end stage is set My children.

All of time as you know, it is being done away with now. The end is come, the end is come, the end is come! Believe it not My children? Prepare ye the way of the Lord. The rider on the white horse is appearing in the skies. See Me not? The armies of the Lord are marching now not out there somewhere My beloved children. I say wake up, wake up and again wake up. A supernatural awakening is stirring all over the land. Take the blinders off My children and be a part. I long for you to walk and flow in the fullness and the anointing. Catch a fire in your bosom, for you are coming through this dry spell and with victory in your souls."

4-26-2013 "Beware The Time Is At Hand"

Hearing this word from the Lord: "Prepare ye. Watchman sound the alarm. The trumpet is sounding, for My people surely sleep. The enemy attacks are on the rise and will only get worse. Do you not know My children the sound of my voice? ***"Battle cry to your stations weary ones. This land is coming down."*** America did not listen, My people, as there was once a hope for her, but she departed and mocked My name. Blood will be in your streets. Think this is a pleasant word? Think again, My children, My people. My servants truly do warn you, for I have them to, but many do not have listening ears anymore. The cares of the world have struck many and they have turned aside. Ye who are asleep in Zion wake up, wake up, wake up!

I know your footsteps that did use to walk in Mine, but ye turned. Did you not think the heart of your God did break when you turned aside and did leave my pathway my little ones? Now I am calling you back and preparing you for the days ahead. Battle cry again do I say to your hearts. Don't you hear it? Wake up My sleeping people. Times are fixing to get rougher than you have ever known, but yet I say if you dig deep into Me, you will go through smoothly. ***"Did you not know I can give you joy unspeakable in the midst of any storm?"*** Repent and come back to your first love. Read it as it is in My word, My daughters and My sons.

Rev. 2:1 "Unto the angel of the church of Ephesus write; these things saith He that holdeth the seven stars in His right hand, who walketh in the midst of the seven golden candlesticks;

2 I know thy works, and thy labour, and thy patience, and how thou canst not bear them which are evil: and thou hast tried them which say they are apostles, and are not, and hast found them liars:

3 and hast borne, and hast patience, and for My name's sake hast laboured, and hast not fainted.
4 nevertheless I have somewhat against thee, because thou hast left thy first love.
5 remember therefore from whence thou art fallen, and repent, and do the first works; or else I will come unto thee quickly, and will remove thy candlestick out of his place, except thou repent.
6 but this thou hast, that thou hatest the deeds of the Nicolaitans, which I also hate.
7 he that hath an ear, let him hear what the Spirit saith unto the churches; to him that overcometh will I give to eat of the tree of life, which is in the midst of the paradise of God.

This word goes out to whosoever will. It is to all a strong warning of what is to come. Some are watching and praying, some are not. Know the sound of My voice as I always leave My people with a hope. Yet I say on: "If you do not heed My warnings, you will not make it through. Dig deep again My people. Love you I do and I am surely coming back for a blood washed, redeemed people. My bride shall be clean and spotless white. I am getting her ready for the days that lieth ahead. Battle weary so many of ye are, but yet I say no time to get out of the fight. Plunge on in after you get another breath.
You see, My chosen ones, oft times you need to pull aside and take a breather, a rest in Me. What does that mean? Get fresh manna from above and bask in My presence even more. So many err at this point. They come out for the rest and fail to join the army, the fighting force again. They go **AWOL** so to speak. **You must stand.** I am fixing to pour out My glory upon the land. Yes, My glory My little ones. At the same time, death and destruction everywhere upon this once great land, but a hidden manna and revival for others.

Two camps, make up your minds. Which one are you in? Come back, come back, come back I speak again. Let the unbelieving depart. Let nothing or no one detour you. I have spoken and that is thus saith the Lord your God."

5-28-13 "Body Without A True Head"

Hearing the Lord speak: "The people are many times hearing a wrong voice in the churches. They are operating not from Me, but of their own control, their own will. Jezebel spirit is in domination is what I am speaking, My children, My beloved ones across the land. It is coming down. A body without a true head is truly what I am speaking to you about. ***"New world order is coming into effect."*** The prophets of old are going to face the prophets of Jezebel that operate by Baal religion. Nothing will be as before.

As the new world order is being set up, My beloved kingdom is rising up in new strength, ready to take the land.

A time of revival is here and a strength will be known that has never been before in My churches. ***"The head will tell the body what to do in My true church."*** I only have one people, not a divided, separated schism. ***"Denominational walls are being done away with. Connections are being made with others of like mind."*** Feast on My word, My hidden manna. Speak My word, My people and be done with it. Know ye not that I speak not a divided word? I give My people truth and have you to stop dividing asunder the Holy Scriptures and applying your own understanding.

"Scripture interprets scripture in light of other scripture, not by any private interpretation. *"* Study it out. Eat of the hidden manna from on high. Guard your tongues well, ye that dare speak against the true prophets of God. I give them instruction and truth of what is coming on the land. Mark My words well and know the difference between Baal religion and the true worship of God almighty. Move higher in Me My children or know of a surety I will cut you asunder. Play games are surely over. I have spoken and that is thus saith the Lord your God this day. **1Kings 18:31** "And it came to pass, as if it had been a light thing for him to walk in the sins of Jeroboam the son of Nebat, that he took to wife Jezebel the daughter of Ethbaal King of the Sidonians, and went and served Baal, and worshiped him."

10-9-2012 "Bricks Are Falling On Your Head"

Thus saith the Lord: "The bricks are falling child. Write it down. Tell the people what I mean. As you yield to Me and cry out like never before, I am pouring out the oil and wine upon you My children. Know you not just as I visit for your sins when you draw nigh to Me and seek Me with all your heart, I visit also with My power bricks? It is the tangible anointing child you are feeling upon you now. The anointing falls like gold bricks upon your head. Many feel it about you but you also feel it about many of them. The favor of God is upon them and you are drawn to them like flies are drawn to honey.

It is the sweetness you feel about each other. It is the last days and as such, I am visiting with My sweetness upon My children. Did you not know that sweetness is in My very nature? Of course the great God of the universe that created man in His image is a sweet God. I have many sides, as so many of you know. ***"Confine Me not and limit Me not in your minds and beings and you shall eat of the good of the land."***

In My vast universe I am pouring out My goodness, My sweetness on who will let Me. As I say in My word, it is the anointing that breaks every yoke. It is a harvest time, a victory time if you may. Just as I last sent strong warnings through this sister, I now send the sweet. As I delight in blessing My children, I speak on. Those who completely sell out to spread My word shall know no lack. I bless you in every way My children. I always provide for your needs. As the anointing gets stronger and stronger upon you, many more shall oppose you. They understand it not and as satan is a thief and liar, he sets out to steal from you and lie on you. ***"Know persecutions will get stronger, but know too the anointing that is upon you will be so strong, many will yield to Me. People need a hope and you have it My children. Deliver the goods."*** I say on: the anointing is not for personal gain but to set the captives free. I tell you a secret. I love you My precious children. You already know that? Ahh... I smile here. Of course you do but you have no idea what realms of glory you are fixing to be took up to. All you need to do is pay the cost and yield to the sound of My voice. Bricks of gold spiritually are falling over many of your heads I say again. I pour out My love unto you this day. This servant hears the sound of My voice and delights to write My words. Try the spirits and see if this refreshing not come by My hand? Delight in Me and nothing will I withhold from you, My blessed children who pay the full cost."

10-28-2012 "Bruised, Broken, Battered-I Am Relieving"

Hearing the Lord speak: "Going through the fire child? Yes you are; for you and many others right now are very bruised, broken and battered. Suffering you are, but yet I am greatly relieving your suffering as you turn unto Me, the great I Am that I Am. I see all and I know all. I have you to tell the people I know what others have done unto them also. Many are under conviction and suffering from My mighty hand, for the things they have come against you in My children. I bring My chastisement on them for hurting your hearts. Did you not know I am a jealous God and My anger is stirred upon the ones who have come against you? Do you not remember I said in My word to touch not My anointed and do My prophets no harm? I visit many for their coming against you I say. They have unfaithful ways and pull back from coming unto the fullness. Many of them even are in the faith, but they do err. I speak on, for the battle has been fierce against many of you as of late. People can only wound your heart when you have let them in. Beware. It is a new day a new season and with the fulfillment of My promises comes a fresh attack from the enemy. *"I speak a strong warning to guard your hearts. Again I say to guard your hearts."* Satan is out to devour you and will stop at nothing to put you out of commission. Allow it not, for with the great travail many have gone through, there is a new strength that has arisen within you. Many do not even know it is inside you, yet but you will soon know. All the trouble and tribulation will seem as nothing when you press on to higher grounds. Grand views await you I say unto you. You are climbing into a place of beauty, safety and a much needed rest. Scale the city walls. I say climb the walls and not only reach for the top, but go over and possess the land. Milk and honey await you. Know for all your faithfulness in obeying My voice, you shall begin to see greater sights than ever before. Plod on and go higher in Me. Some have even now come to the place in Me that there is no desire to turn back. I will see you through all trials all tribulations and when you get to the Promised Land, I say it will be worth it all. Cross on over. I say it is time. Worship Me children in the beauty of holiness. Proclaim My name and praise Me so that no rocks will ever need to cry out. Love affair we have together. I love my children fiercely and I will protect you ever. Guard your hearts little ones, I speak a final time."

9-22-2012 "Call On Me, Now Is The Time"

Thus saith the Lord: "You want to come closer, you can. It is all about choices. I have you move forward only if that is what you want. Do you not know yet My people, that I desire to give you the best? I speak from heaven and I speak clearly. Gone are the days of confusion but only if you walk in My spiritual realm. I visit you with more truth My children. ***"Seek deep truth always and walk in the spiritual realm from above."*** Know ye not there is another spiritual realm? It is from beneath and many walk in it. Yet I speak words to open your understanding further. You cannot fluctuate between the two and have peace. Did you not know yet My children that knowledge is increasing? The mark of a true man or woman of God is to know Me and My ways. Learn of Me and go further. We talk about the wheel again here. It comes down. ***"There is a pattern unto all things My children and I draw it in your lives. In the old did I not speak***

*often of the pattern of the tabernacle? You have to have
one."* A pattern has to be established, a template if you please.
You make all things according to that pattern. It is life I say. I am
molding and shaping you to fit this pattern and some of you yield
not. Another analogy is the potter's wheel. When you are pliable
I can mold and shape you more easily. The great potter knows
how to carefully keep remodeling and reshaping the clay till the
vessel is no longer marred. I am perfecting you, doing away with
sin in your lives if only you let Me. Deep truth you want, you
learned, deep truth you shall get. Never settle, but obtain the
prize. I am the pearl of great price. I take you another way now.
When a fisherman is straining to find the pearl of greatest value,
he gives all to obtain it. He cannot waver or it will not be found. I
am calling you forth My beloved children, for time shall be no
more shortly. It is being done away with in the hearts and minds
of my children who seek Me with their all.

*"They no longer desire the world but have My mark upon
them. Translation comes then. All do not translate. Most do go
the way of the grave."* Why all not seek Me the way the few
have? Get so close to Me, My children that you know you are
being translated and will not have to see death ever. I speak even
more, deeper and clearer unto you. Get your head out of the
sand, My beloved children. Come unto Me and learn of My ways.
Some are seeing these great truths, but yet many are blinded by
satan's lies. I uncover. Mark your paths well and seek My face
more and more. Some are on shallow ground but some are
walking on holy ground. What do I mean? A few are in the
deepest secret place with Me. You are receiving revelations and
understanding. Just as you delight in Me I also delight in you.
I honor you my beloved. You will go to heights you thought
impossible and soar with Me. Others need to climb higher while
you still can. You see My children, this is a transition period and I
am calling unto the deep to go even deeper and be hidden in Me.
You see you can get to a place in me that satan's power cannot
move you in the least. All fear will be gone. Get there My
children. Now is the time. *"The new army of God will have no
fear."* Move out. Marching orders are being given. All My
children can come up higher. Support the weak and help them

up. Don't climb alone. Are you on the winning side? Then act like it. Blow your trumpet and sound the alarm ye mighty in battle. Get on fire and ye will be able to withstand all that is coming on the earth. The plagues are being poured out on the earth. Later? No I say now. Repent of anything hindering you and come up higher this day in Me. I love you My children every one and long to bless you and take you to greater heights. Soar free in Me."

8-27-2013 "Called Forth For Such A Time As This"

Hearing the Spirit of the Lord speak: "The end has come. All things are at hand. War is in the land already and many know it not. Gunfire explosions are in the streets. Violence is in the land, in the courtyards, in the gates and I speak it is only the beginning. *"Wake up My people!"* Many need to do the work of an evangelist and get out in the highways and byways and I will use them surely. Whatever the calling I have placed upon your lives, I am preparing you. I am sending you out amongst the people. *"Leaders arise for you are a special chosen vessel."* Trouble is in the land and it is waxing worse. Prepare to stand and to encourage My blessed people. I always leave My people with a hope and dessert them not. Ye who are called to this appointed time in Me you will hear My voice well if your heart remains steadfast in Me.

"Stand up and be counted for the kingdom of God's sake." Reach the people with the gospel of peace chosen ones of battle and valor. *Be restricted.* What do I mean my little ones? Pull back from the plate, from the people, even at times when I speak it unto you. Empty your vessels and I will fill you with manna from on high. I am bringing you into a new place in Me, My beloved daughters and My beloved sons. Get off the bandwagon of self-pity and grow up in Me. Even My leaders need a special word of encouragement this day. For I say unto your hearts that the adversary has rended you sore and sought to destroy you, but I speak on: "Rise up for a mighty refreshing is on the way and you shall see many things come to pass shortly that the devil

sought to hinder and that is thus saith the Lord your God this day." Be not ashamed of Me before this wicked generation, for I will adorn you with My glory if you only hold steadfast. At special times just consecrate yourselves anew. I want to equip you to lead and speak many things unto My beloved's hearts. I delight not to bring trouble on the land, but this country will be dealt with by My mighty hand. ***"Still will My leaders lead many out to safety."*** Hear Me well and live. Bask in My presence, for I am leading you out of a stagnant place many of you and equipping you well to do the job before you. Be aware, the enemy is trying to trap and blind sight many of you on a matter. Listen not to his voice for he speaks a false report and many do go astray listening to him. ***"Try the spirits and see if what be spoken is of God. My sheep do hear My voice and another will they not follow."*** Lift up your standards, a holy standard before My people. Be gatekeepers and watchmen on the wall. Be wall builders My beloved people. Be peacemakers for then I am well pleased. I love My children to walk in harmony with one another. Division and backbiting do I hate. Encourage one another's hearts, for many of ye strong are ready to quit and throw in the towel. Do it not, for I am speaking unto you to arise and be workers in My kingdom. Little children, love one another and stand as one voice in My kingdom. Mark a person who is constantly causing division and separate from them and allow Me to work. Many things I do put back together in My timing, but I must first deal with their heart. Wait on Me in all things, for obedience is of utmost importance. Fare ye well and know that I have surely spoken this day."

7-30-2012 "Come Closer Unto Me"

Thus saith the Lord: "Idol worship is trying to take over the land. How being you may ask? By people bowing down and worshipping and serving other idols. So I have it to be so? No I have it to be not so, yet many people hear not the sound of My voice. I have all to come to the foot of the cross for repentance. Worship Me only and follow no other Gods. I am the only true and living God and Me alone shall you serve. Know ye not that I am coming back for a righteous people? Many in the land serve their idols and still try to follow Me as well. It will never work. Anything put before Me is an idol My children. I have you come to Me in the fullness and not waver. The time for distancing yourself from Me is over. I call you back to My loving arms. Many in truth and in spirit do worship Me. I know My sheep and My sheep do know Me and the sound of My voice. I will honor their faithfulness. Just as you delight to bless your children so do I Mine. In these last days, I am pouring out more of My anointing on My children than ever before. A mighty sweeping revival is taking place. Be a part. Why wait you? Hear the sound of My voice now and know I am visiting My people with fire and brimstone? No Holy Ghost fire. The righteous know the great move has started. There is a great move in the land and nothing shall stop it. It will intensify as time goes on. To Me there is no time, only eternity. Soon time shall be no more for I am coming back after My children shortly.

Why hesitate some of you to walk in My fullness? I am bringing My people back. Some are being purged, some have already been through the great purging. I purify My people. Come in the fullness I tell you time and time again. How you do that? By letting go of this world and its goods and following Me. Care not what others think of you, for I make a new creature out of you. All things become new in Christ Jesus. I the Lord am visiting your houses and bringing judgement. Some have My blood applied already. You all have fallen short of My glory, but I am a merciful God. As I bring the holy fire, speak My words to others. Share with all and do not be afraid of lack, for I your God do supply all your needs according to My riches in glory.

Let the home fires burn. Stir up the gifts that lieth within you and encourage one another's hearts. Many miracles you shall see, I tell you before and I tell you again. The angelic visitations are increasing across the land. There are many you have entertained that have been angels and you knew it not. Try the spirits My children, for I speak of this in My word. Glory is due to My name. The love I feel for My children is being published all across the land by My messengers. I am a God which can be touched with the feelings of your infirmities. Many need to grasp My heart. Do you want to know the heart of God? *"I am love and even though I have a side of Me that pours My wrath out to the disobedient, it grieves Me."* The very essence of My being is love and to know Me is to know love. When you come into the fullness, you will give yourself totally to go where I lead you and even say you are not your own anymore. *"Many say that now but it is only lip service.* If you care to go further you may, My blessed children. I always bring you closer if only you yield. Great treasures are stored up for you even now, you know not of. Eye hath not seen, or entered in your heart all that I have prepared for you. Your mortal mind and bodies cannot bare it now, but you shall be changed, in the twinkling of an eye at My great coming. Then you will know as you are known as My holy word says. Rest easy My people and be not deceived by satan and his devices. You shall reap if you faint not. Fare you well and be a blessing to others always. I close with My great love by the hand of My servant this day."

8-12-2012 "Coming Home"

Thus saith the Lord: "The love of money is the root of all evil of that I speak to you often. The truth is coming out, for many of you shall examine your hearts to see if you be in the faith. Write to the people, blessed are the ones who die in the Lord henceforth and forever. Some have coveted after money and erred from the truth. When they go to get their reward, they already have it. What do I mean? They put it in a bag with holes and I blow on it. With what? My wind. *"My spirit is blowing now across the land thus saith the Lord."* Ye are a people after My own heart, yet many are corrupt in their ways and doings. An unrighteous seed will not I accept. Beloved, cleanse your hands. Ye double minded, think pure thoughts. Remove the rubbish from your vocabulary. I am coming back after a holy people without spot or wrinkle. My people shall be pure, for I have called them to righteousness. The ones that heed My voice will I repay; goodness for the fruits of their labors. They are blessed in the fields and blessed in the harvest, for harvest time has come. ***"It is now My people. Stand steadfast. I stand at the door and knock. Won't you let Me in?"*** I love My people. Many of them go astray after Baal. I say follow not after them. For you are My beloved, adorned as a bride for her husband. Now rest children. For I will speak further My child. The rest are coming in. I have decreed unto you same as for them. For the ones who have stood steadfast, have I brought their loved ones, for such a time as this. The prodigals are coming home, My children. Think not I have seen your hearts, when you have cried to Me for your wayward children and loved ones? I love you with an everlasting love. Of course I move on your prodigals to come home. They are getting tired and weary of their ways. Rest on, for I reveal more. Love the people, serve the people, bind up the broken hearted, for My end time army must train others. Equip others to fight, not to lay on the side lines. Gird up your loins and march forward. Be on the move for I am shaking the kingdom. Tenderly I speak this day. Be at peace."

10-28-2012 "Death And Destruction In The Land"

I speak unto My people: "Many of My chosen elect are sharing with you what is coming on the land. I have you to believe My prophets, but still always try the spirits. Deception would creep in if you are not careful. You need a stronger sense of discernment, many of you. Call out to Me and I will give it unto you. Trouble, trouble, trouble is ahead. What does it take to get your eyes open My people, I say unto you? I have visited a long time this nation, but still they don't repent. What was once a godly nation is now serving idols. Think you not I visit for your sins? Still I say on: "There has always been a remnant and there is one even today. The power of the holy people has been scattered, I say unto you as the book of Daniel speaks on. It is going to take much perseverance to make it in these last days. You must look unto Me or you will be much disillusioned. Come

apart My people and get a second wind. For many of you are tired and weary and need a refreshing. When you get battle sore, you must look up unto Me and refresh your weary souls. You must always look unto Me, the great I Am, but there'll be times when a pulling back from all around you is needed. I'll be enough I say and can put you in overflow, if only you yield unto Me. I give a warning here. After the refreshing, forget not to get back in the battle. Destruction is in the land and the only key to making it through, is to hear My voice and obey Me thoroughly. Partial obedience will never work. Remember Saul. Although he was anointed king, he lost his position for not fully obeying My voice. *"In these last days it is imperative to keenly listen."* With all the destruction here now and coming soon to what was once a great land, I will deliver you to safety. Did you not remember in the Old Testament that there were what was called *safe cities? "If I move you to a spot, then stay there till further command. I have set up My children to help you and will not leave you without a hope, in the midst of destruction and tragedy.* "Does it delight Me to bring all this vast destruction? If you think so, you do not know My heart, My people.
How can many of you be so long time with Me and still not know My ways and nature? It is a heart of love, not wrath I wish to pour out, but this nation will listen no other way. This very nation is being brought to its knees by My hand. I speak on. *California* is soon to know My great wrath. Still I have you to pray for the people. Because of your prayers that I hear, some will be spared. Wake them up My children. Sound the alarm, blast the trumpet and spare not with the words I give unto you. Still make sure that you speak only My words and mix not your own into it.
That is how close it comes, My beloved children. *"I speak again to constantly try the spirits. When you are close enough unto Me, you will know truth from fallacy."* I close with tears running down My servant's cheeks. She feels many of your pains and walks the floor for this nation, as many of you do also. I give you hope and see you through this troublesome time. Keep trodding on the right path, My precious ones and believe not a lie. *"Love you my church I surely do, but the error of America's*

ways has come up as an ugly stench in My nostrils."

12-7-2012 "Discern Or Try The Spirits"

The Lord speaks: "The love of the Lord is in your hearts, many of you, but yet you hesitate at times. Now is the time to gird up your loins and press into My kingdom. Sometimes it is hard to press your way through, but that is where I can give you an extra measure of grace. You will need it in this end time. For surely I say unto you, to call on Me in the day of trouble and I will deliver you and you shall glorify Me. Think I do not stick with My word? A sharper sense of discernment some of you need. Watch the words of the prophetic being delivered across the land. I have a **signature**. My little ones who recognize My voice know I sign all My words spoken. *"The prophetic must always match with My word or I say, just throw it away."*

Be not deceived by man no matter who he or she may be. I have a **pattern** and I stick to it. Truth is heard in every syllable and it will always line up with scriptures. I draw you closer not further away. Even though My words sometimes are a chastisement, I will always leave you with a hope. That is the key, My children. *"When anyone speaks in My name, at the beginning and the end, you will always see My great love."* A loving father does chastise when it is needed. Gird up your loins I say again and press in. A false word will glorify **man,** that is how you will tell. Give not place to putting your approval on it. Seek My face, My children and listen for the sound of My voice.

I will reveal further. Judgement is in the land, but yet some are whitewashing everything. The love of God, the love of God is all they preach. Yes, for surely I am a loving merciful God, but there is also a judgement side of Me. *"Watch a person and mark them who supposedly flow in the Lord and never bring a chastisement."* Know this My people, for I surely rebuke and chasten who I love. Many false are in the land and speak great swelling words and I am not pleased with them, for they lead My people astray with their easy believism. I say on: "Judgement must surely begin at the house of God. Repent and move up higher in Me. You have not arrived yet from the least unto the greatest of you. Loving kindness I am pouring out all across the land. It is truly to a remnant do I speak. ***"Do you hear Me? Then listen to My heartbeat."*** I love every one of you but many will fall if you don't gird on new strength. Hard times are ahead. Still, more glory will be poured out on this generation than ever before. Press in and press on. Forever mark those that cause division and separate yourselves."

9-20-2013 "Do You Want To Know More About The Wheel?"

Referring to **Ezekiel 10:12-22** heard in the spirit: "The wheel is coming down daughter. Explode it, My explanations over these verses. Start with verse twelve.
12 "And their whole body, and their backs, and their hands, and their wings, and the wheels, were full of eyes round about, even the wheels that they four had." A wheel, a wheel, ever a wheel. Four wheels going and intertwined with one another. What is that about daughter, My beloved children? Who are these creatures? I am talking about the cherub, the man, the lion, and the eagle. Go back to the beginning first, which is the ending you say. What does it say here? The 'eyes' were this way, that way, looking around, all over the place. Looking down over the heart of man. What were they seeing? Disobedience, plain and simple. Where at? All over the place; across the land, across the nation, across the world, I say unto you. Men repenting not of their evil deeds. Where is this at? **Revelation 5:3** also.
3 and no man in heaven, nor in earth, neither under the earth, was able to open the book, neither to look thereon. Yet you say, this don't make any sense. Think again, for I say it does. I opened the book daughter. All eyes shall see. Each one to their own opinions? Yet I visit the land for their wicked sin. Still I call forth repentance, but it will be too late one day. My hand is still stretched out to a wicked and perverse people and generation.

Come forward, yes, My people and I will reveal a matter. I dwell in the thick darkness. Why do I say that? I am everywhere, all across the land even now, seeing what I can see. Are there any that seek after righteousness? Come out from amongst them live separately and I will receive your daughters and sons. *"Meaning rend your heart and not your garment unto Me."* Now we will go forth and I will explain about the four creatures. Take one at a time--the cherub, man, lion, eagle... (To be continued at a later time, as the Lord gives unto me and leads. As always, try the spirits.)

11-14-2012 "Eat The Whole Roll"

"This is given to My chosen elect. You will know if you are one. Observe what I say unto you and not only lay it to heart, but do it. I speak in My holy word, these words. **Ezekiel 3:1** "Moreover He said unto me, son of man, eat that thou findest; eat this roll, and go speak unto the house of Israel.
2 so I opened my mouth, and he caused me to eat that roll.
3 and he said unto me, son of man, cause thy belly to eat, and fill thy bowels with this roll that I give thee. Then did I eat it; and it was in my mouth as honey for sweetness.
4 and he said unto me, son of man, go, get thee unto the house of Israel, and speak with My words unto them.
5 for thou art not sent to a people of a strange speech and of an hard language, but to the house of Israel;
6 not too many people of a strange speech and of a hard language, whose words thou canst not understand. Surely, had I sent thee to them, they would have hearkened unto thee.
7 but the house of Israel will not hearken unto thee; for they will not hearken unto me: for all the house of Israel are impudent and hardhearted.
8 behold, I have made thy face strong against their faces, and thy forehead strong against their foreheads.
9 as an adamant harder than flint have I made thy forehead: fear them not, neither be dismayed at their looks, though they be a

rebellious house.

Revelation 10:7 "But in the days of the voice of the seventh angel, when he shall begin to sound, the mystery of God should be finished, as he hath declared to His servants the prophets.
8 and the voice which I heard from heaven spake unto me again, and said, go and take the little book which is open in the hand of the angel which standeth upon the sea and upon the earth.
9 and I went unto the angel, and said unto him, give me the little book. And he said unto me, take it, and eat it up; and it shall make thy belly bitter, but it shall be in thy mouth sweet as honey.
10 and I took the little book out of the angel's hand, and ate it up; and it was in my mouth sweet as honey: and as soon as I had eaten it, my belly was bitter.
11 and he said unto me, thou must prophesy again before many peoples, and nations, and tongues, and kings."

So you think this word not apply today just the same? Think again My beloved children. For I am the same I change not. I call who I call and choose who I choose. Many of you must prophesy before people even of other tongues and nations. You must get ready. Now is the time. Thou hast set out to do a work for Me. I see that. *"My all seeing eye sees everything."* I spoke to thee that thou must eat the roll. Many of you have not done it yet, but in part. This child ate the whole roll a long time ago. She tasted the sweetness in her mouth as honey and the bitterness was in her belly.

Now some of My chosen elect must do the same. Meaning children, some of you have only given out My word in part. You are holding back. That is because you have not come altogether in the fullness. I am ready for you to go further in Me now.

"Partake of all of Me." Give out to the people My words and My words only. Know ye not that the end of this nation as you know is now here? It is being brought down by My mighty hand. Trouble is in the land and I warn you over and over by My servants that it will only wax worse. Still there is hope. It is in Me and you will prosper even through this time if you only obey My voice. Did you not know that there can be peace in the midst of a storm and a mighty calm in your soul? I am speaking to My leaders in this message. Prepare, prepare, prepare and again I

say prepare. Not only for your own houses to be watchmen over, but to many others, you are called. Do you want the blood on your hands? Speak only My words, not your own. ***"Eat the roll and be consumed with all of Me."*** You will never be the same and will deliver many I say unto you. To the ones of My chosen elect who ate the whole roll, I speak a word unto you. Lead the leaders, for all have not come into the same place as yet you have. Judge them not, but guide and lead them. My word will never return void, but it will accomplish that which I set out for it to do. Be consumed upon my altar of sacrifice all of you. Love you I do. Eat the roll."

7-16-2013 "Encouragements To Your Hearts From Father God"

Heard this in the spirit this night as was seeking Him: "The great God of heaven and earth that made all is by your side. Every power from on high has been channeled for either good or evil. Know the difference. Exercise your faith and your gifts. Let no opportunity pass you by. Know good from evil, My children, I speak again to your hearts. I am calling many in these last days to take a greater stand. ***"Stand or you will fall I say unto your hearts."*** When a person arises within your area that seems to have true spiritual power, try the spirits. To many of you seeking My face, I am sharpening your discernment in these last days. You need it my beloved. Your walk must be true and you need not closely connect with others that have not the same vision and goal. Many have a false spirit and only pretend to love Me.

Warfare, the battle is on and going to get hotter. Draw nigh to Me and I will see you through all things. Surely I say unto you, as you draw nigh unto Me, I will feed you from manna from above that the world cannot partake of. Greet the dawn. What do I mean My beloved children? As you get up in the morning, seek My face. Get on the offensive instead of the defensive, My little ones, well beloved ones. Many of you have been beaten almost to a bloody pulp by the enemy. I am raising you back up in these last days.

You do not know anything yet. The great God Jehovah speaketh a word unto your hearts. ***"As you yield to Me, the glory bells will be ringing. I am bringing you into joy unspeakable and full of glory. Your God loves you. Never doubt it for a moment. In times past you may have faltered. Your weariness made you fall and pull back. Not anymore I say unto you. Now is a new day. I say unto you it is 'summertime' in the natural for many of you as well as in the spiritual. No time to pull back, for the enemy will get an advantage of you."*** Yeah I say further: rest when it is time and you are battle weary but get back up. I tell you before I tell you again, many surrender at this point and give up the fight. You are needed, you are loved in My kingdom. Did you not know I delight to lift you back up and encourage your hearts? Shake off the discouragements by praising Me. Do you not have something to praise Me for little ones? ***"Count your many blessings and know I am calling you up higher."*** I have spoken and that is thus saith the Lord your God this day. Believe and know I will turn things around for you. Only keep your eyes fastened on Me. Rest in Me, My beloved children."

8-11-2012 "False Prophets"

Thus saith the Lord: "With fire in your bosom ye shall prophesy as of yesterday same as today. Beware of false prophets, for they come in sheep's clothing. Pretending to love the people, they devour them. Many tried and true have I yet, but more of the ones who seek to devour My people. Blessed are ye child, for you shall understand further. Each one who lines up against Me, prophesy in My name, when I send them not, I will destroy. By their fruits you shall know them. I am coming back and My reward is with Me when I come. Many to destruction, some to life everlasting. ***"Yes child, the way you shall know them, if they feed my people."*** False prophets are ravening wolves inside. They wear the sheep's clothing, but My people need to beware. Sheep they are not, but ready to take your money and all you have. A true prophet of God lets the Lord lead you and is not after filthy lucre. True it takes money in My kingdom to operate. For the things in this world are not free, yet they beg and plead not. They lay it out there and leave it to God to supply the need. Empty and broken are they many times. Still I come on the scene and take care of them. ***"I would not have you rob the prophets. It is of great importance you hear Me. Feed not the false in the land."*** Discern the spirits when they cry self. Self it is not of Me. Balance I have you walk in. My people need to learn of Me. For a tender God, I am and full of great love and mercy. Reject Me not My people, for I am coming soon. Blessed are ye who listen to the words of this prophecy. The rider on the white horse is fast approaching. I AM He."

6-7-2012 "Father Speaks A Two- Part Message"

Look in the <u>1st chapter </u>of the book of <u>Haggai.</u>
Know ye it not where in the <u>6th verse </u>it says? "<u>Ye have sown much, and bring in little; ye eat, but ye have not enough; ye drink, but ye are not filled with drink; ye clothe you, but there is none warm; and he that earneth wages earneth wages to put it into a bag with holes.</u>" Hear the sound of My voice well, for I will speak on. Get out of your bed of do nothing and I will receive you. As you ask of Me, I shall give you the desires of your heart. Are they holy desires? I have them to be. What do I mean? Garnish your wages again I say. People, you have no understanding. Some of you do in part I say. I open your eyes further to the truth. You put stock in the things of the world. Your money bags have holes in them. How do I know? For I send you back empty and broken every time. This is a two in one message. Hear it well. The learned will search it out. Where am I sending you to? ***"To the cornfields for they will receive you. It is simplicity am I talking about. Back to basics, the beginning. I have you know truth. I shout it in the heavens."*** Repent, trouble is in the land. The false prophets are in the land, so are the true ones. How do you tell the difference? The true always leads you closer to Me the false to themselves. Take no glory for

yourselves My people. Rise up and be counted in My kingdom army. There is a great onslaught of evil taking over the land. Hear My voice well. Gird up your loins be strong. Fight like men and women of God. Know ye not the sound of My voice again? I repeat the matter. The false are in the land. The false take over. How? By you not hearing the sound of My voice. Big time ministries are coming down. Not all of them but some of them; the money hungry ones. I am coming back soon and My reward is ever with me in my hand to give you. Truth is what I reveal. Partake of Me, all of Me and know the difference between right and wrong, truth and error. Baal and false religion is coming down. He is feasting on his own bread. It is the anti-christ system. His reign of terror is over. How? By rising up and being counted in My kingdom.

Hear ye well, My people. ***"Take his kingdom down. Be not overcome of evil, but overcome evil with good."*** Fear not his voice. He reigns with terror and controls with deceit. He puts fear in man's heart. It is a system, a world system and the harlot, the whore is sitting on the beasts back.

Revelation 17:3 "So he carried me away in the spirit into the wilderness: and I saw a woman sit upon a scarlet coloured beast, full of names of blasphemy, having seven heads and ten horns." What do you see? Look at it from new light. It is truth. You can only break the walls of unrighteousness down by praise. Pure and simple. Do you want leanness of soul or fullness? Search it out. Rebuke Baal by hearing My voice well. Baal is the false, the world system, the world's ways. Harlotry is her game and she is deceitful. She will catch you with her eyes. ***"You men, beware of the woman with the roving, winking eye. She will blind you, she will deceive you. She has always brought a man to a piece of bread. Resist her smile, her ways. She will destroy you."*** It is a spiritual it is also a literal meaning. Beware. ***"Woman guard your doors against the enemy. For men will try to consume you, rule over you with a rod of iron. Protect your fortress."*** Marry only when I tell you. Be equally yoked, not unequally yoked. Let the latter rain fall children. Guard your heart well and live. My words are signed sealed and delivered to you this day. Hear Me well and that is thus saith the Lord."

11-11-2012 "Feed My Lambs"

Thus saith the Lord your God: "Feed the hungry hear their sounds, My children. Surely it is for spiritual food they need. Feed them My word. The word sanctifies and it is holy. There are many who are yet not able to eat meat, but are on the milk bottle. They are My little lambs, but surely I love them too. Know ye not this? Give them food fit for their little stomachs. My lambs are not able to devour meat yet. Do you not understand My children? You need not criticize them but strengthen them. It is my job to increase and grow them. Yet some refuse to grow, but I will deal with their hearts. Many still be on a bottle and need this type of nourishment for now. They are babies. Would you give babies strong meat? Of course not. ***Feed them food gentle for them to digest and I will surely do the rest.*** I will be well pleased. Fare ye well."

12-31-2012 "Focus, It Is All About Focus"

Heard the Lord speak: "Focus, it is all about focus. Gone are the days of wine and roses. Some of you have thrown your heart away for a song. Cheap it is not and a heavy price you have paid. I say give not your heart to another in the romance department unless first I endorse it. Hear the sound of My voice my children. Many have been rended by loves sweet song. I say come apart and be revived and refreshed in Me, My daughters and sons. Is love not available? Is it not comely to hold someone close to your heart? I say yes and no and we will explore. When a person is enthralled with another, their thoughts, attentions are centered on them. Is that not right? I say naught. ***Your main attention and focus should always be on Me, first your Adonai, your king.*** Then if love comes, put it into its proper perspective little ones. If you put Me first in all things, it will work out most times.

Why do I say most times? There can be a flip side. Time is right and time is wrong for some. Events and circumstances have gotten in the way. Hearts hurt, hearts are broken even many times when I have sought to put things together and bring it about. *"Sometimes your beloveds choose wrong and do not hearken unto Me in the design of it all. Then you surely need to move on."* Your pain comes upon you sharper than a knife cutting you. Breathe I say little ones... Breathe. You think I do not see that pain My little ones? Again I call you little ones, for surely you are My children, My beloved. Bruised and battered many of you still are, yet I am healing and binding you up. I have you lay them on the altar of sacrifice and move on, I say again. Now we will explore the sweet side. Many times you have been hurt and wounded so bad, you just feel like giving up on love. Do it not. Seek not for another, be whole in Me. Yet, do you not think that sometimes I desire you to be with another to fulfill My kingdom, My furtherance of the gospel? Surely seek, implore My face about everything. Time is too short in these last days to falter. When you are whole in Me and come together with someone of like mind that I have given you, it is a wondrous thing and brings much glory unto Me. Just have My stamp of approval on it. Always do know I have you not unequally yoked, for two can never walk together unless they are agreed. I never go against My word. End time army is marching forward. I say those that have a wife be as those that have not. You want explanation for that, I will give it. Hear, hearken unto My voice. Put not your wife and her desires above Me. Be godly husbands and lead with dignity and strength. Never rule over with an iron rod, for you will crush the heart of a tender woman. Still many a man has been browbeaten with his wife and lost his focus. They give place to her and when she is not spirit filled, it hinders My design for what I seek to accomplish in their union. Two need to walk together side by side. *"Love should rule in a marriage. Two with one heart, one purpose, to fulfill My will in their lives; unconquerable a picture, example of Christ and the church, my beloved bride. A union from heaven it can be, if only you let me put it together."* In these end times, entire nations are crumbling. It is a time like never before. That is why I start, begin with don't lose your focus My children. Give not place to the flesh. If a man cannot contain, it is better for him to marry than burn. That is what My holy word says. Still if he chooses because of his strength in Me to remain unyoked with another, so be it. He will be as a eunuch. His focus, his eyes are surely fixed on Me. ***"So if you marry, praise Me, if you stay unyoked, praise Me."*** Let nothing divide your heart. Marriage is honorable in all and the bed surely undefiled. Love can surely be a sweet song in its proper perspective putting me first. Still, whoremongers and adulterers I will judge. I have spoken."

 1-7-2013 "Forgiveness And Completeness In Him"

The Lord speaks: "Many of you are wondering what to do about this, what to do about that. The decisions are weighing heavily on your minds and hearts. Did you not know My children, My little ones, that I see the beginning from the end? All things will work out in the end as I have ordained your footsteps, your walk. Scarring, we will speak about it now. So many times the enemy has rended you and your heart hurts bad. People have come against you and circumstances have oft ripped you apart. Move on, I tell you, but first you must bring it all to Me for your healing. ***"Did you not know that I care about the little sparrow that falls to the ground? Surely I care for you My people, My little ones. The very hairs of your head are all numbered."*** "When the enemy has hurt your heart, it brings pain almost unbearable at times. So many times you look at the person and blame them. Even many a time, it has been a friend, beloved, who rended you. Surely they were a tool of satan, a pawn in his hands and they did not even know it or realize it. Unless a person is sold out to evil, most times they are not even aware of how much they have hurt you. Remember you have done likewise at times with others unbeknownst. ***"Forgive easily and quickly."*** It is a new season and one wrought with many a decision. Choose right and only as I move on you to go forward, My little ones. New steps are you taking and the enemy would desire to divide and conquer you as he has done in the past. Forgive quickly I say again and bring the offenses to Me. Let Me put the forgiveness in your hearts for that does not even begin to lie in you. It is by My mercy and by My grace you even exist. Only in Me can you forgive. Get the slate clean, for you cannot start a new year with old things holding over your head. This is most important for many things must be made right in this new year to move ahead. Focus I speak again and again through My prophets. It is all about focus and I do say consecration unto me. Let nothing or no one break your focus from Me. ***"I am bringing you into a deeper experience and the hindrances must surely be done away with."*** I am moving many of the old people out of your life, as far as a close walk together. I am arranging others for you to walk with and bring into your paths. It is destiny. This is surely a year of destiny of many things being fulfilled, you have waited on for a long time. It is all about faithfulness also. Let nothing or no one turn you aside. Consecrate wholly unto Me all things on the altar of sacrifice. Resist not and cry out to Me in everything. ***"Discern the spirits for that is most important."*** Let a lot of the old things go that have staggered you. Get not so hung up on trying to figure things out in this new year and hold not on to offenses, I do speak again. My will, My design little ones. I have spoken and surely I will perform all things well."

3-22-2013 "Get It All Right Before My Altar"

"It is a time like never before My children, My little ones. I see your hearts, how many are longing after My return, My second coming. I am well pleased with you. Continue on in the faith, operating only in My grace, mercy and truth, I do say unto your hearts My beloved, My little ones. I speak on: "At an altar of sacrifice, many have surely laid it all down, never to look back. I am well pleased. Yet to many I would speak a warning once again. You are still walking in pride, stiff-necked before My face. Think I do not see it? Think I do not want you to bow the knee, which is symbolic of the heart, My little ones? Yeah, I know many physically cannot bow, but your heart can be rended unto Me. I speak on: it is recorded in My word, that surely all will bow their knee before Me one day and they certainly shall. I ask you this question My children, My little ones. Where is the proof in the pudding as I oft speak about? Sweetness is what I mean, for I say many of you are not sweet, but still have bitterness in your very souls, and truly I am not well pleased. Get rid of it. Bring it all to Me. At an altar you must lay it all, to be fit for My kingdom. Correction time, for I speak the fruits of the spirits must operate and flow in you My children or you will be stagnate and put on a shelf eventually, if you do not yield to the sound of My voice. What do I mean? I am bringing sharp correction to this people through My servant and she would rather post the sweet, but will hearken unto My voice and deliver this word. It is time and past time to make things right, for I am wanting to use you in a greater way in the days that lieth ahead. I will not use a unclean vessel and many of you are drawing back and have let pride slip in again. *"This is for all from the least to the greatest of you to examine your hearts. If the shoe doesn't fit, no need to wear it I say unto you."* For I say on: it is needed and will help many, My child. I never leave My people without a hope and only rebuke those I love and chasten. Guard your tongues, for surely some would speak amiss. Know you not it says in My word, that out of the abundance of the heart, the mouth doth surely speak? Speak words of life, words of victory and I will be well pleased. I have spoken."

9-9-2013 "Give Us Lord Our Daily Bread"

Heard this word of the Lord: "Can I set a table in the wilderness? Who doth prevent Me, My beloved children? Know ye not trouble is in the land, but I your great God of glory from above is in all places, all times. I rule and reign and scatter evil with My very eye. Provide the scripture daughter. Look it up. **Prov. 20:8** "A king that sitteth in the throne of judgment scattereth away all

<u>evil with his eyes.</u> Who am I? The great King of glory, that is who. I can do more than a mortal king who reigns could ever do. Daughter, beloved one, give My people My words, My encouragement from your Father's heart. Many have come against you in the past, My little ones. Think I do not see what has been done? They have hurt you much. Think I was standing on the sidelines when it all happened? No for surely I was there. It was only 'training grounds' and all things did bring about My purpose My daughters, My sons in My kingdom. Love Me, serve Me and make peace wherever possible with all mankind. ***"Still wait on Me for My timing and seek for reconciliation."*** Many things that have been sorrowful to your hearts are changing. I am re-aligning many of you to walk together in peace and harmony in this present evil day. What the enemy sought for evil and to bring you down I use for only good in the final analysis. Know My voice. Move in My timing and be exalted on high. If you seek to exalt yourselves you will be brought low, My daughters, My sons by My mighty hand. Yet if you seek My face and humble yourselves, there is great reward My people. I will move you to higher grounds and that is thus saith the Lord your God this day."

8-4-2012 "Glory Be To God"

Thus saith the Lord: "It is of the Old Covenant, I write. Never would you have known My love if you had not known My law. It was the schoolmaster to bring you to Christ. You are of a chosen people, a royal priesthood of that I speak further. Many of the times you have called on Me in the night and I have been there. Where were you when I made the heavens or parted the red sea? I reveal a mystery to you. The church is about to go through great tribulation like it has never been before. I have you be prepared. How? By putting on all of Me. Clothe yourself in My righteousness, purity of heart and soul and put on the whole armor of God. Rejoice not in iniquity, seek not revenge on anyone. Love Me like never before. You are brought into such a time as this. Hear Me well, for I speak through My servant the prophet. Your time has come to walk in the fullness. I say now. No longer put it off. Gird yourself, for the battle is on. It is going to get hotter. Still I pour out My anointing to all who listen in a greater way. Lean not to the left nor to the right, take no side roads for I come on the scene. I am with you to walk every step of the way. It is a straight and narrow way you follow children. It is a plain path and does not have the glitter of the world, but yet I abide on the walk with you. *"Obedience is better than sacrifice and if you come to Me now, you will avoid many pitfalls you would fall into."* Your ways are not My ways thus saith the Lord. That is why I draw you closer, so you can hear the sound of My voice. What is holding you back? Is it wealth? I own the cattle on a thousand hills. Seek not after money, but if you find it, use it for My kingdom. Still many needs you shall have supplied also. What is a dollar? It is twelve cents. What do I mean? American currency has no value anymore. Seek not after gold that can corrupt, but after My kingdom which shall never be destroyed. Nuggets of truth are you receiving from this sister, yet from many others also. She is not the only one. My prophets are all ways through the land like a mighty army being raised up. They speak the same word I give them. Mark them that cause offense and division is what I speak. There are many false prophets in the land. They tickle your ears. What I have you to do My people is come closer even now, for I speak on. Sick, suffering, defeated many of you are, but I am coming on the scene delivering My people in this hour. Bind up the broken hearted ye that are strong, for there are many hurting out there. Religious spirits cast out and perverse ways. You have to be a clean vessel for Me to use. This child is a pure vessel or I could not use her. She is willing to pour out to you, for she feels many of your pains. Trust Me for more child. She gets weary sometime getting a word for you, but I refresh her quite well. Tell them it is of Me that I speak to them of a positive way this day. I know when My children need a sharp word, or a gentle one to encourage and lift them up. Speak on this day, for many are listening, more than you even know. Trust not in the flesh My children. I tell you this before. It will lead you astray. Learn to listen to the sound of My voice. I speak to the inner man and I get to the heart of the matter. What do I mean? It is in the heart whereby are the issues of life. Out of the abundance of the heart, the mouth speaketh. What is in man that I should be mindful of him? He is of My creation. I made Adam out of the dust of the ground. What about Eve? To walk beside him as she came out of his rib. I love you My children. I seal this word with My love."

9-12-12 "God Is Greater"

Your God speaks this day: "Just as this sister is in overflow of the Spirit, so are many of you. I have told you before, count the cost and some among you have done that. I speak words of encouragement unto you. Once again flow in My Spirit, My anointing and I will give you rest as you need it. There are times when you set aside everything and everyone and just praise Me. These are troubled times, but glorious times as well. "***Pay the full cost and nothing shall be withheld from you.***" Fare ye well and love you I do. Go forth and sing My praises and live and breathe in Me."

5-28-2012 "God Reveals For Our Benefit"

(The Lord spoke to me that Baal was the spirit of divination and it is all across the land.)Thus saith the Lord: "Take the blinders off and you shall live. Get off the totem pole. You are too high My people. Learn of Me and My great truths. Know ye not the sound of My voice? As times before I will speak to you again. Let me in. Know the difference between false and truth. My word is truth and I have hid it in the heart of all who believe. Want to follow me? Then believe my report and live. Say ye not the burden of the Lord no more and I will receive you. Revelation comes to all who believe. That is understanding with your eyes open and clear vision. I have you My people not deceived. The prophets of Baal are out there. *"It is the prophets of religion.* **They are**

many." Still are there more in your camp than in theirs. Theirs is a master of deceit, a web, if you please. Garnish your wages I say. What do I mean? Put not your wages in bags with holes, for I will blow on it. Know ye not it is in the book of **Haggai**? Read the book. Ye learned study the word. It is in the **1st chapter** of the book of Haggai. Know ye not where in the **6th verse** it says?

"Ye have sown much, and bring in little; ye eat, but ye have not enough; ye drink, but ye are not filled with drink; ye clothe you, but there is none warm; and he that earneth wages earneth wages to put it into a bag with holes." Hear the sound of My voice well, for I will speak on. Get out of your bed of do nothing and I will receive you. As you ask of Me, I shall give you the desires of your heart. Are they holy desires? I have them to be. What I mean? Garnish your wages again I say. People you have no understanding. Some of you do in part I say. I open your eyes further to the truth. You put stock in the things of the world. Your money bags have holes in them. How I know? For I send you back empty and broken every time. This is a two in one message. Hear it well. The learned will search it out. Where am I sending you to? To the cornfields for they will receive you. It is simplicity I am talking about. Back to basics, the beginning. I have you know truth. I shout it in the heavens. Repent, trouble is in the land. The false prophets are in the land and so are the true ones. *"How do you tell the difference? The true always leads you closer to Me, the false to themselves."* Take no glory for yourselves My people. Rise up and be counted in My kingdom, My army. There is a great onslaught of evil taking over the land. Hear My voice well. Gird up your loins. Be strong. Fight like men and women of God. Know ye not the sound of My voice again? I repeat the matter. The false are in the land. The false take over. How? By you not hearing the sound of My voice. Big time ministries are coming down. Not all of them, but some of them, the money hungry ones. I am coming back soon and my reward is ever with Me in my hand to give you. Truth is what I reveal. Partake of Me, all of Me and know the difference between right and wrong, truth and error. Baal, false religion, is coming down. He is feasting on his own bread. It is the anti-christ system. His reign of terror is over. How? By rising up and being counted in my kingdom. Hear ye well My people. Take his kingdom down. Be not overcome of evil, but overcome evil with good. Fear not his voice. He reigns with terror and controls with deceit. He puts fear in man's heart. It is a system a world system and the harlot, whore is sitting on the beasts back. It is **Revelation 17:3** "So he carried me away in the spirit into the wilderness: and I saw a woman sit upon a scarlet coloured beast, full of names of blasphemy, having seven heads and ten horns. What do you see? Look at it from new light. It is truth. You can only break the walls of unrighteousness down by praise; pure and simple. Do you want leanness of soul or fullness? Search it out. Rebuke Baal by hearing My voice well. Baal is the false, the world system, the world's ways. Harlotry is her game and she is deceitful. She will catch you with her eyes. You men, beware of the woman with the roving, winking eye. She will blind you, she will deceive you. She has always brought a man to a piece of bread. Resist her smile, her ways. She will destroy you. *"It is a spiritual it is also a literal meaning. Beware."* Woman, guard your doors against the enemy, for men will try to consume you, rule over you with a rod of iron. Protect your fortress. Marry only when I tell you. Be equally yoked, not unequally yoked. Let the latter rain fall children. Guard your heart well and live. My words are signed, sealed and delivered to you this day. Hear Me well and that is thus saith the Lord."

June 2012 "God Uses Who Will Let "

Yeah thus saith the Lord: "My children, I speak through My servant the prophet. In My kingdom are many mysteries. I have you to know them. My children that hear My voice will seek Me and be lead of me. I guide you on a straight path. Narrow is the door and the gates are wide open for you to come in. Know ye not the sound of My voice? Understand not My mysteries being revealed? It is a kingdom matter. To the book of revelation you must go. I am searching for a perfect heart, a willing vessel to use in My kingdom. I am hungry and thirsty for you My people to come in. I have called you for such a time as this. Yeah I will speak further: I use who I use. The lowly who are called have a mark on them for this end time hour. I am revealing much to My servants. A day of wrath and judgement is upon you. Yield not to the flesh, for I am judging your houses. Many shall come forth in this end time hour to obey the sound of My voice. Get in or out and that is thus saith the Lord. Fooling around with you no more am I. Straighten up your lives, for I will visit America not many days hence. Know ye not the sound of My voice? I repeat again for you are in error. It is appointed unto men once to die and after that the judgement. Repent quickly and I will receive you. Who is this going to? Whosoever will. Be not dismayed for your time is here. Many are walking in righteousness and hear Me. To them I will say, well done my good and faithful servant. Get on the firing line prepare for battle and receive Me. What do I mean? In your homes, in your lives, to all things, do I want to be a part. March forward, take no steps backward and keep yielding. Why? Because the day is coming when all you know now will be gone. In My visitation I am leaving a remnant who will not turn back and hear only the sound of My voice. Get ready, for the battle is upon you. I warn you My people. But with a warning, a blessing. For if you should turn from your wicked ways, great and manifold blessings are and will be poured out upon you. Your families are coming in, great dilemmas are solved and a great refreshing is filling your house. Of what do I speak? Your tabernacle of which you do dwell. ***"The revival is sweeping the land be a part and good things are in store for you and that is thus saith the Lord."*** I put before you this day a curse or a blessing. Choose you this day whom ye shall serve."

8-14-12 "God's Peace"

Thus saith the Lord: "Through the portals of time, I have called you My children. Do you not know the sound of My voice yet? What this is about? I am renewing hope in the hearts of mankind.

Many of My children have fallen but surely I am picking them up. Sadness has been part of satan's plan long enough. Sure you are sad at times, when things touch your heart of evil that has come on the land. Still you must think it through. Evil will not be part of My plan. Yet as I told you before, mankind chose wrong. One day I will wipe away all tears from your eyes. Is it now? It is soon and my visitation now is getting stronger upon earth than ever before. Hear the sound of My voice and abide in Me. There is a new day fixing to dawn without any evil in it. I have come back many times to gather My children to Myself and delayed it. Why I do that? My people were not ready. I tell them time and time again that I am truly coming back after a spotless church without spot or wrinkle. Gather them in My children. What do I mean? The more you yield unto Me, the more anointing do you walk in. Others see it and then many will begin to desire to have what you have. It makes them hungry for more of Me. As you move forward and let Me speak through you, others resistance to the truth is broken off. ***"My anointing will flow greater than ever to the ones who seek Me in the fullness."*** Is your heart's desire souls? Then let Me pick up the broken shattered pieces of your life and use you in My kingdom. Fare ye well and look up, for your redemption surely draweth nigh. Be at peace with yourselves and one another. I have spoken and love you I do."

6-22-12 "Harvest Time Is Now- Reap What You Have Not Sown"

Our Lord speaks: "Empty and broken have you come to Me many times and I have always come on the scene. Give out to this people. What? My love and My admonitions. The time is now. Harvest, children for I come soon. Glean what is in the fields. Prepare for the reaper. I bring many souls into the kingdom of God, rejoicing with Me that someone reached out to them. Why do you tarry? Know you know that I am coming soon and then it be too late to gather them in. Souls are dying spending an eternity in separation from Me. Care ye not? Weep not for yourselves but for My people which are not saved. ***"Know you not it is for them I died? Care not I was crucified on the cross for the sins of the whole world? It was a bloody cross of cruel rejection. The pain I bore no one can know."*** What is a soul worth? In eternity they will spend it with Me or with satan in a burning hell. Get on fire my people; for I care others are perishing. Trust not those that care not for others, for they walk to the beat of their own drum, but My people know My voice and follow Me. Blessed are ye My child for writing these words, for I see your heart crying out for souls and souls you shall have. Would all Gods' people desire souls as you do. You will once more get on fire for Me, My people, for I do all things needed to bring this about. Ye that fight and resist shall receive the greater damnation. Ye chosen ones shall hear this message well and take heed, for my servant delivers it with tears dripping down her cheeks. I never close My word to My people. Your words of comfort to Me do I hear also My people. Do you not know I call you for fellowship and intimacy with Me? Press on for more child, I will reveal more. Tell them it is of a sweet fragrance I smell of a few. I'll not leave you comfortless. The comforter has come to abide with you."

8-19-2013 "Hear The Sounds"

Thus saith the Lord: "Hear the sounds? From the beginning I have called down to man and he listened not. Many stopped up their ears, but a few opened their ears. What sounds I am talking about? The sounds of the universe calling out to you My children. What that is about? Listen you shall hear. Holy hush, hear it? What more? My thunder booming and lightning crashing. Think you cannot hear lightning crashing? Think again my beloved, for I take you on a journey you have never been. The earth is crying out in travail to be delivered. Many can hear the groanings. Wake up the ones who have never heard the sound. Also, there is a baby crying in the universe. What that is about? Many of the babies born are not wanted and I have you hear it. Keepers of the gate are you watchman on the wall. So I desire for you to learn more of Me, pure and simple. Some are reading this and think you are in the fullness. ***"To be in the fullness you would not think that. For I tell you time and time again till you weary me. You have to always be going deeper in Me. You can never arrive till you get home."*** So quit thinking you can figure it out and come inside the holy of holies with Me. You say you are there, yet you come and go. I have you stay and then you will truly know of whereof I speak. Fare ye well and I speak to your hearts one more time. My stamp is upon you and My beloved you are. Yet I yearn to show you greater heights that you have ever been. Love you I do. Now get on fire stay on fire and know I will see you through all your troubles and trials. As you get above the clouds in Me, you will never look back My children. I desire all good things for My children. I close with My love unto you."

12-11-2012"Hound Dog Religion"

I had a vision through the night meant to be shared, I believe. In this particular vision, I had seen an old fat 'hound dog' with pieces of paper stuck all over him. They were destinations of where he had been. The Lord spoke: "Hound dog religion is taking over. Stupendous events are taking place all over the world. The dog carried baggage. What does that mean? Poor sad hound dog, traveling everywhere laden with proof of ownership of where he had been. He packs them in-the crowds. The events are one after the other. He is broken down, abused, lonely and destitute but yet he still keeps trodding on. Who is this hound dog and is he howling tonight? Remember the song Elvis sang about him? Useless old hound dog never even caught a rabbit. Now tell me, how could he have even ever tried to be his or your friend? He couldn't and he can't with you either. Religion of the world is off balance I say. Religion can never be your friend but is your worst nightmare, your enemy. I say on: partake of the world and its religion and you will get sick every time. It is simple. Read the word. ***"Pure religion and undefiled is to visit the widows and the orphans."*** I keep it simple and the world complicates it. World religion does not care about you. They lift not one finger to lighten your heavy load. Come apart My children, I say unto you again and again and I will receive you. Babylonian system is still howling! Your choice I say unto your hearts. Choose wisely."

11-17-2012 "I Am Reeling Them In"

Hearing the Lord speak: "I speak a special word unto your heart concerning your children this day. Some are even your grandchildren, who have been gone astray from the fold. You have long waited for them to come in. Stalling and walking on uneasy grounds are a lot of them. It is a brand new day and I speak I am dealing with their hearts. ***"The ones who have been in rebellion have my hook in their mouth now. I am reeling them in."*** Excited in Me have many of you been, but have suffered many consequences for your choices I say. There has been much separation in your families because you chose Me. It has brought division in your families for surely the cross separates. I speak on: you thought your children was not watching your lives, but surely they have been. Even though they have witnessed many of your mistakes, they could not help but see your steadfastness in Me. Some have even been puzzled what has kept you going with all the trials you have suffered. Did I not promise to bring them in? Turn around and look at where you are at my beloved. ***A new day is here.*** Hold on for many sad situations are beginning to turn around. Things that have broken your heart are about to be mended. Hold on, I say again for you are right at the door of breakthrough. Joy unspeakable and glory abounding is what is here. Keep your eyes straight ahead, for your prodigal children and grandchildren are coming home. To some of you I do speak about spiritual children you have begotten through the gospel. Same with them. Keep sowing seeds of kindness, for you are causing many more to be hungry for me also. More spiritual children shall you have as you continue on in my goodness and mercy. Nurture them I do say. Closer must they all come and you are fixing to see the manifestations of many things not many days hence. A faithful God am I. I don't play My children. *"I speak not only about sin but neither do I play with My children's hearts. I deliver I do say unto you."* Some of your beloved ones are already in My camp, but are being drawn closer unto Me. Think I cannot make front line soldiers out of them? *"Begin to praise Me and rejoice for it will set things in motion."* Evil assignments are being canceled off them as you cry out unto Me. I have heard those cries about your beloved ones and write you a victory note this day. Believe not the devil's lies anymore, for I am lifting up your heavy hearts. Think I not see when you cry for your little ones in the night? Think I cannot visit them in the hog pens? Think again. With the new day dawning lies greater responsibility. To much is given, much is surely required. Be consumed completely on My altar of sacrifice for there will you find Me. I am longing to pour out My love unto you, for I am surely all that your soul could ever desire. I give only good and perfect gifts. Stir up the gifts that lieth within you, support the weak and climb on up the ladder. Be sure to always take others with you on the upward climb. As you get closer unto Me, many things will begin to be unfolded unto you. Many mysteries are in My kingdom. I will reveal as you seek My face. Your little ones are coming home I say again. Love you I do."

6-11-12 "It Is Time For Your Healing"

Thus saith the Lord: "Tormenting spirits are coming down. Relief is in the camp. What do I mean? Deliverance is yours if you only believe. What? My truth for it is in the book. The book which you read. Take it all, rightly divide the word of truth and be done with it. Get out of the forest. The trees have blinded you long enough. What I say? A whisper in the wind or do I speak clearly? All the time do I speak to your heart. Let me in and I will perform all I set out to do in your hearts and lives. Hurting? To Me must you come. I have the solutions to all of your problems if only you believe. Believe what? My word. I have spoken it all between the pages of the book. Get on fire and stay on fire. I am using My children in this generation like never before. Arise to the call. It is a call of arms. Gird on truth, get on fire and take Me to the people. It is a spoken word now sent to you from My hand delivered to you by My servant the prophet. Know not her? She knows you and recognizes you well. I reveal through her. Many recognize the gift I have put in her hands. It is to get you closer. She is underneath you all, yet for she serves and is only wanting to please Me and not man. The truth remains to this generation that I am coming back soon and My reward is ever with Me and it is in My hand. I forget not My promise to come and get you. Get on fire, receive no evil report, but a true word. My promises are yeah and amen. I guide you in all truth. Now is the time to move out. Never look back but go forward. Listen children, for I tell you your deliverance cometh. It is to yield and to ask Me to consume the dross in your life. Bring Me your pain, not to man but to Me. Know you not that I made the body and the mind? I know how to heal it all, which are the torments that lay inside you. Call on Me in the middle of the night, cry out and say I am holy and I will fix your pain. Know ye not I care about your pain? I died for it, for you had no way to get to a holy God but by Me. I died for your salvation surely, but I am after the whole package; for I want all of you, then I relieve your suffering. Now you understand? Jesus Christ was born of a virgin, knew no sin, but yet died on a cruel cross for your sins. I am coming back to relieve your suffering. It is now.

It is not in bodily form I come at this time, but in Spirit for God is a Spirit and all that do worship Me, shall worship Me in Spirit and in truth. Don't deny Me access to your throne room, which is your heart, for I long to dwell there. Now we get to the heart of the matter, which is let Me in to the deepest innermost place of your heart. It is a place you don't even want to go. For when I go in there, that is where real cleansing begins. Flow with Me and through Me, My children. What do I mean? I am cleansing your vessels as you yield to Me and I put it in you, so you can flow out to others that they may be healed. ***"The anointing, My children, for it is the anointing that breaks every yoke."*** Want to be set free? Hear the sound of My voice and yield. The peace that surpasses all understanding shall fill your hearts and even your minds. For I am a great healer of the mind and I can put peace within you. ***"Tormenting thoughts are not of Me, so dismiss them quickly."*** Never entertain them, as I am of peace and the comforter has come to reveal truth. Blessings to you My people this day, for I write you a good word, a comforting word, for I bind you up, where many have been broken. I love you My children and tenderly do I speak this day."

6-6-2013 "Light Or Darkness"

The Lord spoke to me this word: "Get the blinders off My children. Darkness is coming upon the land. Noon day I say unto your heart will be as dark as midnight, soot soon. It is a spiritual meaning My daughters and My sons. ***"Light or dark-- which one do you want?"*** Darkness is taking over the land in America, this once great nation. Already events in secret behind closed doors are taking place. Arise soldiers of the cross and lift up your royal banner high. Put on your battle gear and declare the word of the Lord. Are you ready for the onslaught of evil? ***"Know ye not that in the middle of the battle; the heat, I am building a church that will never bow down to the enemies commands? My church shall stand strong."*** A blood bought remnant shall be spared and many of your loved ones, for you have called out for mercy to Me in their behalf. I hear your cries oh ye of little faith.

"Think My heart is not moved when My children cry out to Me in truth and in spirit?" Control, many are trying to control and manipulate you. It is time to lay aside all heavy weights and hindrances, as I send my people, strong warning in this land. Quit straddling the fence. Decide for time is short. Battle lines are clearly drawn. My sheep hear My voice and will not follow another. Regiment command... Forward march... You want the truth or a lie? The devil, the enemy, will certainly send you deception. Clean your ears out of the spiritual wax My people. Read my book, the holy bible. Increase shall ye have as ye seek my face. Let nothing detour you, for you are needed in the rebuilding of this once great nation. As it falls, great will be its collapse. It's infrastructure is weak, toppling even now. Still I will have mercy on who will let. *"Call out unto a holy God, for I will hear your cries even now My children."* Why pine ye away for the world, for the things that would cause you to fall and be a stumbling block? Seek after Me and My righteousness and ye shall not be moved, My children. Ye shall eat the good of the land. While the children walking in disobedience and darkness are betraying others to death, some shall taste of **hidden manna** in these last days. ***"Your cup shall surely run over. Great increase in My camp, My daughters and My sons."*** Revival fires are spreading and I am visiting in the land. I will send you out. Many of you are on a journey and hence why the heat has been so hot. You are being tried and tested in the fire. Call on Me in the day of trouble and I will surely bring, deliver you out. Fare ye well little ones. Take My warnings to heart, as you will be used mightily of Me, if only you let and yield all to Me. Speak daughter and publish My word to the people. Thus saith the Lord thy God this day.

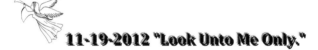

11-19-2012 "Look Unto Me Only."

Thus saith the Lord: "Cry out unto me now My children. Don't wait till the storm begins to howl more. You need to prepare now, I do say unto your hearts. The fierce winds are beginning to blow, but know ye not I am a shelter in the midst of a storm? Seek refuge in Me only. Again I do say, wait not until things are spinning out of control. Many storms of life have you been through. Yet nothing but My great mercy shall prepare you for what is about to take place in this land. Do I write you a word of fear and trepidation or hope in the midst of despair? Of course the latter. Now prepare I do say. Look at it another way now My beloved children. When a soldier knows which way the enemy is coming, he does not have to duck. No he can do an all-out attack. Get on the offensive, for the battle is on. ***"Look not to the right or left, don't turn around on the road you are on, for it is short and narrow. The only one who can walk it with you is Me."*** You must walk alone, for no mortal man can walk your walk for you. I carry you at times, did you not know? Sometimes you are not even knowing how you made it through a place, but looking back you see it is I, your God that carried you. I will see you through and with great victory in your souls, My children. Only look to Me. I Am that I Am. (Coming back after note was written-I was puzzled why the Lord spoke the way He did, that the way is 'short and narrow'. I try the spirits just as everyone should always do when receiving a word.) **Mat. 7:14** <u>because straight is the gate and narrow is the way, which leadeth unto life and few there be that find it.</u> He spoke to me: you are closer home than ever before child. The road surely has been long. You are nearer home I say again and the distance is shorter now. Keep plodding on for the sights of home are just ahead."

2-6-2013 "Lusting For Power"

Hear the Lord speaking: "Lusting for power; the world is lusting for power. Here a little there a little, till you be taken out of the way. What does all that mean children? Get the scripture out, I will reveal. **2 Thes. 2:7** <u>"For the mystery of iniquity doth already work: only he who now letteth will let, until he be taken out of the way.</u>" Greed, it is about greed My children. I want, I want, I want. I fulfill the needs you have. I even give you the desires of your heart, but is that enough? To some it is not. You seek a broader way, many of you and you do err. What do I mean? Your eyes are set on the world and it is about to consume you. You have asked amiss to consume upon your own lust. In truth and in spirit, you must come humbly bowing before My face. It is a heart matter. I have you My people, to bow your heart. It is not the position of the body so much as humbling yourselves before Me. I see the heart, I always have. Man looks on the outward, but

I look on the inward. I see the motives inside. I see inside even the joints and marrow of bone. I, God alone, know how you were formed in your mother's womb. Easy believism I say leave alone. Is it the rule book and the law? No guess again. It is grace freely given by My hand. Your redemption cost Me all. All I do say unto your hearts. Do you think that your cost will not be great also? Pay the cost, the full cost, for when you do, you will find in Me the pearl of great price. *"I will work many things out my beloved that have been hindering and troubling you, if you will only hearken to the sound of My voice."* Keep not ordinances that I have not ordained. What do I mean? If it is not of Me then leave it alone. Some ordinances are good and those I placed in My word. I am speaking now of foot washings and the Lord's Supper. Why do I have you wash one another's feet? Because of pride, plain and simple. It humbles your heart. Many have done away with foot washings in this day and time. They declare it was for those back then and because of their dusty trail. It is of now also and I will reveal further My children. It is a humbling act I say again. Come before My presence with singing and with laughter. Now, how will what I say here tie in with this message above? You are about to start on a new journey, My beloved, My children. It is fraught with many a peril, many a danger. End times and all the troubles it brings with it, but yet joy I place within your hearts, if only you will receive. In Me is your peace and life everlasting. Behold My face and live. Bask in My sweet presence and rejoice in Me, not in iniquity. Remember not the days of old for I bring you forth with a new day dawning. Drink of new wine. Partake of Me little ones, all of Me. Partake of My sufferings also. You must walk a godly life, one with My stamp of approval on it. When you partake of the Lord's Supper, know the seriousness of it all. Refer to the scriptures here daughter and let them read for themselves. **1 Cor. 11: 23-31**. It is life unto you if you partake in the right fashion... Death if you do not. Drink and eat worthily my beloved... Made worthy by My precious blood; the atonement for all sin. Now I take you back one more time to the beginning. Lust not for power, but seek My face only and for the holy anointing to be upon you. People will come by and be refreshed often by you, if you will only hearken to My voice. To My beloved ones I do speak and My love is poured out upon you all this day. Only know I am dealing with many of you to draw closer unto Me. For I would speak further this day: those I love I always rebuke and chasten. It is traveling time for many of you. Throw off the weights and sins that so easily beset you. I speak to this child first, my anointed one, to deliver this message. None of you have arrived yet and that is thus saith the Lord. Make all things right. Draw closer unto Me and get all hindrances out of the way. I have spoken."

8-15-14 Meditation On Zech. 14:1-6

(A friend and dear sister in Christ, asked me to seek more from the Lord on these scriptures. Look at what is happening in the Middle East right now, how it is heating up. It sure is time to pray like never before. As always, try the spirits with 'anyone' giving out a word.)

Zechariah 14:1 "Behold, the day of the Lord cometh, and thy spoil shall be divided in the midst of thee.
Heard the Lord speak: "I am dividing the spoil now and people do not repent. A remnant remaineth.
2 for I will gather all nations against Jerusalem to battle; and the city shall be taken, and the houses rifled, and the women ravished; and half of the city shall go forth into captivity, and the residue of the people shall not be cut off from the city.
That is happening now and the people do not even realize it.
3 then shall the Lord go forth, and fight against those nations, as when he fought in the day of battle.
I am already fighting against them and the people are deceived. Then is now and that is thus saith the Lord.
4 and his feet shall stand in that day upon the Mount of Olives, which is before Jerusalem on the east, and the Mount of Olives shall cleave in the midst thereof toward the east and toward the west, and there shall be a very great valley; and half of the mountain shall remove toward the north, and half of it toward the south.

I will come and set up My kingdom and that is a literal meaning. Prepare, for the millennial reign of Christ. Why do they not run to Me now instead of in that day for it will be too late? **5 And ye shall flee to the valley of the mountains; for the valley of the mountains shall reach unto Azal: yea, ye shall flee, like as ye fled from before the earthquake in the days of Uzziah king of Judah: and the Lord my God shall come, and all the saints with thee.** A cloudy day of confusion it is. Again, it is now as well as then. In My kingdom, time does not matter anymore. It is a spiritual as well as a literal meaning. Time is done away with; it stands still and is not. Do you not know My people I inhabit the praise of My people? Gird on new loins and strength this day. Approach Me and I will bring a thing to pass. What am I talking about children? The end draweth nigh. These are end time messages. Let it rain. Let Me reign in your hearts and lives. Then will I pour out The Holy Ghost and fire upon your heads. Give and receive of Me. Flow well in the anointing, and you shall break off many strongholds on the people. A new life I am talking about. The old life is gone. I give you, My people, a breath of fresh air. Receive it and live. Dry bones come to life. Remember Lot's wife. Never look back or you will be left behind. What does that mean? You will be taking steps back into spiritual darkness. Go forward My children and prosper. Guide My people well. You who are spiritual, hear My words well. Deliver My people. Lead on. **6 and it shall come to pass in that day, that the light shall not be clear, nor dark."** Why is that light not clear nor dark in this verse? So the blind can see for in writing this I am explaining as I go. Yield more and I will show you more daughter. The great sickle is put in the earth now. What is it doing? Reaping grains of truth in your hearts and beings. I separate truth from fiction and apostasy from deliverance to spiritual heights attained. What am I wanting you all to do is come closer and hear ye well the sound of My voice. The chosen elect know who you are, for they know who they are. Many have been called from a child, yeah I say even from birth, but this is resonating within their beings as truth. The others will not hear this message. They can't for it is not appointed unto them. What do you do with truth? Proceed further to search it out or return back to the weak and beggarly elements? Your choice, you chosen elect better yield now, lest a worst thing come upon you. The spiritual rightly divide this word.

Now fare ye well, for I close this portion of My word. Later, more will be revealed and that is thus saith the Lord."

4-12-2013 "Migrations Are Coming"

"End time revival is here. Get in it. Be a part of it. Refreshing poured out like you never seen. Yield unto Me and I will give you more. Precious the words are in your mouth. I write them on your heart. ***"Take Me to the people. There is a day coming everything will be gone as you know it now."*** Migrations are coming. People are fleeing ***south*** is what I am telling you and destructions. Holy Ghost rain is being poured out all over the land. Healings are taking place. The lame walk, the dumb talk, the blind eyes see. Every step you take, you are closer to being in the fullness. Precious, the people are not ready, but I am stirring their hearts to receive the latter rain. Empty and broken I am bringing them back. Each and every day, the prodigals are coming home and that is thus saith the Lord. Deliver it to the people. ***"Watchman get on the walls."*** Prepare to blow the trumpet, for the walls are coming down. As it was in the days of Noah, so shall it be in the days of the coming of the son of man. Prophesy to the people. Prepare ye your heart for war. Know child, it is a spiritual battle but it is a physical battle. ***"The troops are coming in."*** Sound the alarm. Draw nigh child. Reach out to Me in love. Your fruits are coming in. Many that have been lagging behind are getting stirred in their spirits. Seal it up. I have you deliver it, but not at this moment. March on to victory."

8-26-2012 "Miracles Of God Or Satan- Know The Difference"

Thus saith the Lord: "Blinders are coming off many of you if only you believe. Know ye not, I am able to calm your storms and give you peace within while you are battling many things? In these latter days, great miracles will be taking place, but be aware and 'discern the spirits'. Did you not know Satan desires to **'counterfeit'** everything I do children? Know the difference. Try the spirits always and see if it be My mighty hand or the hand of the enemy. Know the difference. How are you going to know? There is a distinct **sound** in My kingdom. It is a *tone* and it takes a discerning ear sharpened by Me to tell the difference. Satan is *as* a raging roaring lion, but he truly has no teeth. He only wants you to think he does. Deception is his name and his game. Wake up, wake up, wake up My beloved children. When I do a miracle, then it works for good always in My kingdom and only reflects Me and I get all the glory and the praise. When satan with all his lying wonders performs miracles, all bow down to him and he gets the glory and praise. Wrong my children, for I have My people to come alive in Me and know the difference. (Addition on 3-30-13 that I heard in the spirit:) Satan should never get the glory and praise, yet he often does, for you discern it not right. His ways are wicked ways and many times you discern it not right. New wine are some of you surely drinking. Even so, but you must learn of Me and My ways more. Satan's kingdom is coming down, but you must destroy the strongholds, the yokes off people, I say unto your hearts first. Order is being restored in this day and age. I have you move in My flow and My anointing only. **Quit buying the lie.** Yield unto me, for I am bringing you out of confusion into clear, greater light. Did you not know there are **degrees** in My kingdom, My beloved children? You see a thing and it be true in that aspect, but yet if you dig for *deeper truth'* then I will open your eyes to a greater extent, My little ones. Cry out for more discernment. I am sharpening you for what lieth ahead so again I say wake up and be counted in My kingdom. Love you I do."

12-30-14 "New Age World Movement- Or My Divine Order"

<u>Matthew 11: 28</u> "Come unto me, all ye that labour and are heavy laden, and I will give you rest.
<u>29 take my yoke upon you, and learn of me; for I am meek and lowly in heart: and ye shall find rest unto your souls.</u>
<u>30 for my yoke is easy, and my burden is light."</u>
New age world movement or My divine order? Which shall it be My children? Hear My voice well and live. The Enemy attacks on the land and ye see it not, many of you. Come closer unto Me. Behold My face and partake of My goodness and blessings. There is a place in Me you can get, that will absolve all doubts and fears. Warn the people child or the blood will be on your hands. Many are still sleeping. Wake them up! Rise up in all authority and post My words to the people. You have been hindered in many aspects, but I am bringing you out. Publish My word. Calmness, quietness and strength ye shall have, My people as you seek Me out, above the rush of the world. Let it lay dormant at your feet. You move the hand of your God when you walk in steps of **obedience.** Know it not? I see your struggles your trials and even say all that is going through your very minds. It is a time like never before, even like Job's trials and ye wonder what is going on? I am moving you out, not many days hence and am preparing you for the journey, I say unto your heart. ***"Think I not care about My own and will bring you into that perfect place of obedience?"*** You have been sorely wounded. Take the time to refresh, but then jump back into the battle. Hearts on fire for Me... A perfect place around My throne to sit and bask in Me. It will ***cost you*** but which do you prefer, hearing the world's clatter or My still small voice, which shall give you direction and clarity? Rise up soldiers take on new strength. Get in the meat of My word. It will always correspond to what I say and speak unto your hearts. You are blessed in My sight, but I say come closer to

Me one and all and that is thus saith thy God this day."

7-24-12 "Obedience Is Better Than Sacrifice"

Note: I just wanted to say here, after you read the Word below, to please apply understanding from the Lord. I am 'NOT' out to promote any specific Church or doctrine. Divisions separate, and God is surely bringing His Bride into 'Unity'; 'Harmony' and 'like minds' in these last days. I am simply Christian. Still I must share what I have heard the Spirit of God speak. It is my desire you always try the spirits. That being said, I surely believe in the different manifestations of the Father; Son; and Holy Spirit. The Word speaks in Colossians 2:9 "For in him dwelleth all the fulness of the Godhead bodily."

Thus saith the Lord: "Surely is the day coming when My wrath will be poured out on the children of disobedience. The day is now and I am visiting many already. I have called out time and again to you but, yet some of you still linger in your sins. Know ye not, that I desire to give only good things to My children? Why do ye hesitate? Believe ye not My report? Why do ye make Me use my chastening rod of correction so many times, instead of Me pouring out My great blessings upon you? When you draw not nigh to Me in all things, you wound the very heart of God. Many of My children stop short of total surrender. Children, know ye not that these troubled times you live in, I can see you through? The fire will get hotter for satan knows he has but a short time before My return. He is seeking whom he may devour. I am here now to help you out in all your troubles. You see My children; I walk through your problems with you. I never leave your side, yet when you walk away and do things on your own, you tie My hands. *"Partial obedience is still disobedience. Remember Saul."* It is in the word how he failed Me for a reason, as I love My children and do not wish any to lose their reward. *"I have My reward with Me when I come again."* Know ye not, I come time and again and ye are not ready? That is why I delay My coming. At My appearing, many shall rejoice and I tell you as times before, I am coming back after a pure and spotless church. I have washed you in the blood of the Lamb. I lead you into all truth. I am truth, I am righteousness, I am love. *"When you take on My name, you are complete."* Do you walk in My name or your own? What is My name children? Of course you say it is Jesus and that it is, but many of you stop there. What do the scriptures say in **Acts 2:38**? Repent and be baptized in the name of the Father, Son and Holy Ghost? Now read it for it says be baptized in my name. Quote the scripture child: Acts 2:38 "Then Peter said unto them, repent, and be baptized every one of you in the name of Jesus Christ for the remission of sins, and ye shall receive the gift of the Holy Ghost." I have but one name and it is Jesus. Know ye not Jesus is God? I do not have you baptized in titles. Some of you I have dealt with time and again and you have resisted, even though you see the truth in part. I have you search for deep truth, total truth and be set free. *"When you go under the water in My name you partake of all of Me."* Argue the word? Well, you'll not argue the word with this sister, as she has already seen the truth and it set her free, as it will you if you only take heed. Come before My presence and learn of Me. Search the scriptures and see if this be so. Try the spirits and be sure if you come against this word, you will be coming against truth. I change not, neither do I lie. You are a blessed people and I love you, every one. Be not deceived and take the step I command you to take. *"Truth is truth and a lie is a lie and My children have been deceived long enough."* I will bless you as never before. I visit My people, for many in these last days will see and change the error of their ways. I say Father, Son and Holy Ghost are titles. The name is Jesus and it is singular and not plural. I'll not have you baptized in *titles,* I tell you again. *"Hear the sound of My voice, My children."* In **Matthew 11:28-30** I bring you this word, but many have misapplied the meaning. "Come unto Me, all ye that labour and are heavy laden, and I will give you rest. Take My yoke upon you, and learn of Me; for I am meek and lowly in heart: and ye shall find rest unto your souls. For My yoke is easy, and My burden is light. *"When you search within yourselves and others for answers, the right answer does not come. I have you come unto Me and I will do the rest."* Heavy hearted and laden down are many of you and the troubles of the world are about to consume you. I have My people to be set free. The rule book is thrown away when you fully surrender to Me and I will be your portion and your deliverer in all matters and teach you in the way you should walk. Fare ye well and know that I am a **patient loving God** and I bring you into a **deeper walk** with Me as you only obey Me. I am a God of love and am extending My hand of mercy unto you this day."

4-21-13 "Order Out Of Confusion And Chaos"

"Nothing shall come to pass till people are all of like minds. They must come together, all putting their parts with one another, My child, My daughter. A little bit won't work anymore. Confusion is in the camp; get on board the great ship of Zion, where My great love is poured out My children. Learn to get along in My body of believers. Quit dividing and conquering. I do rebuke your hearts, those that are guilty. Listen to the sound of My voice and live, My children, My little ones. Nothing is about yourselves or should be in My camp. The enemy has set out to deceive and confuse you one and all. Only the strong shall stand and survive my little ones. Truly put all things into My hands. Know ye not I only have your best interest at heart? I see all; I know all, My beloved ones. I will work order out of confusion and chaos, for I am the great God of the universe. Only thou must listen and surely obey My voice. Many are still trying to come in the wrong door and it will never work. You want to figure it out and it is not possible. The cost is great and I say unto you it costs you all. It is not a little sacrifice but a big.

All of your ways you must surrender to Me. It is required. Little bit will never do. You must surrender to Me fully at the foot of the bloody cross, My little ones. Many know of Me but, yet if they do not My blessed will, they never know of My ways. There are great abiding mysteries in My kingdom. Want to know them? Then surely I say, bow before Me your heart and seek My face and I will reveal unto you many things. Did you not know a great mystery is to be discovered? When you leave it all behind and focus only on Me you will walk in new freedom. ***"Know My word is truth and never will I reveal contrary unto it."*** Upon this rock, I will build my church and the gates of hell shall not prevail against it. Get off the totem pole and quit trying to climb higher in the world, saints of the living God. Come up higher in Me and ye shall eat the good of the land. I have spoken."

10-6-14 "Perfect Law Of Obedience"

"Perfect law of obedience. Walk therein.... What is the perfect law of obedience children? Pretend won't work. Do you love Me? Keep My commandments, pure and simple. Are they few? Are they many? What are they? Identify and simplify. Thou shalt love the Lord thy God with all thy heart, soul and very being and your neighbor as yourself. Post it. Love works no harm to its neighbor. If you love Me, you will work together in harmony and peace of the gospel. Get yourselves out of the way. Walk softly together. Humble thyself and move in My atmosphere of glory and praise...Go into the bride's chamber of forever after with your beloved. Know Me in an intimate way, secret place and courts of love. You have heard My voice. Now march together in unison."

5-31-12 "Put On The New- Off With The Old"

(The following is a word to Me after the Lord was letting me feel only a little of the pain that he suffered on the cross. I wept and wept as I was feeling the nails in my hands; the thorns piercing down on my head; a beating on my back. I cry now to remember how much more I fell in love with my Lord and Savior! I know I shall ***never*** be the same. ***"This happened by degrees over a several week period."*** It was so intense the pain, and I could barely stand it! I feel truly what apostle Paul must have felt, when he said in **Gal. 6:17** "From henceforth let no man trouble me: for I bear in my body the marks of the Lord Jesus.") "So you want to partake of Me? Then partake of all of Me. Partake of My sufferings. Crown me with righteousness, majesty and glory you say, but first remember the sufferings. I abused you not, but revealed the great pain I endured for your sake, but yet I withheld My hand; for you would not have been able to withstand the many sufferings and beatings of the body I took, nevertheless, the pain I took with the nails piercing My hands. ***"Take Me to the people now."*** See what I mean? A suffering Jesus, but a whole Jesus do I present unto them. It was to the joy set before Me did I endure the cross, despising the shame. I am not on that cruel cross any more, but yet still I suffer from My people. How you say? ***"By ye not yielding to the sound of My voice."*** Come quickly and obey Me, for I will feed you with the good of the land. Take the next step. Cross over Canaan land is your discovery. How to get there, you know not. Food for the journey? Patience, endurance, temperance, majesty, beholding great splendor on the trip and last but not least, kindness. Partake of My all. Where at? Around the throne. I am clothed in majesty. I reveal a matter. Want it? Come closer to Me and ye shall hear the sound of My voice. What is it saying, My voice saying? ***"I love you My people and I will endure the trip with you, as it is an uphill, upwards climb. All the way you shall see beauty."*** Joy is in your souls... And why do you stop? You see pain and suffering. What's that about? The enemy is about to bring you harm, but yet I do you good. How is that? All he meant for evil I meant for good. ***"Watch your mouth. Guard it closely for you have entered into a joy season."*** It is a new birth entered into from the sufferings you have endured. You have a right My people. You have endured, many of you the test, now you must endure the storm. But wait I see a new horizon. Perched on top of the hills, is a new day energized with many victories, wholeness and quietness to your soul. Write it down, write it all down, for I am writing on the tablets of your heart. With a great battle cry have you called out to Me. Now, eat the good of the land. You have a right to it. Partake of the spoil. Glory time awaits you all. New heights, new depths, new victories do you enter into this day and I have signed, sealed, delivered it in your hand. Beware of the enemy. He is out to steal your joy. ***"He has*** *no place in your life but is a trespasser."* Get him out. Beware, beware, beware of his traps. They are deceit, confusion and most of all lies. Draw your swords, pierce his wicked sides, enter into the enemy's camp and bring confusion and that is thus saith the Lord. Polish My word to them child. Meaning smooth it out. Fine tune your instruments, for I am bringing you into a new day. Now walk in it. Glory awaits you. The old is passed away, behold all things become new. Get on fire. Stay on fire and I will receive you and that is thus saith the Lord. Now publish My word. Get out of the way and I will use it to perform all I set out for it to do. For many are hungry and thirsty for a new word. Child, this be one of old. Praise Me and I will come on the scene. All glory is Mine. You will receive, for I share with you. All I have, you shall have too. *"Abide in Me and know ye not the same cup I drink out of you shall drink out of also?"* Rest in this. Not a moment too soon have I come on the scene to share this with you as many have fallen across the land. Rescue them, preach My word, and deliver them by the power of My might. I have spoken and that is thus saith the Lord. Feed My sheep and live for they are a hungry, scattered sheep. Gather them in now and that is thus saith the Lord."

6-2-13 "Relationships Of Every Sort"

Hearing from the Lord: "I speak unto your heart child, daughter to tell the people, move on from a person when I say move on. What is the heart of the matter? Many times a person in a relationship is not ready to come closer and give it all. Life has wounded or stabbed them too much and they refuse to move on. Their choice it is where to fully love again or not; plain and simple. What did I tell you as you awoke? Write it out child, daughter. A person must be willing to touch the very heart and soul of the other, when I bring you into close alignment with them. It hurts, the pain of being rejected. Still, why did I allow it to happen, even seeking to put it all together? You see, when I closely link, bind two together, many benefits comes forth for both parties. It broadens you and it broadens them and brings them one step closer to being free if only they let. I make no mistakes; let me assure you My children.

Romans 8:28 "And we know that all things work together for good to them that love God, to them who are the called according to His purpose."

I bring out the best in both and I bring out the worst, for I am teaching My dear ones to get along and to some I do closely align. Conflict issues will always occur, for I your God do bring all things to *light*. It is always best for those to sit down and talk it over and out. I have all My children to dwell in peace amongst you if at all possible. Sometimes it is better to just soar alone I say unto your hearts my little ones. When a person does not yield before Me to get fixed with their hearts, it surely will then hinder you and stagnate your growth. It allows Me to work and fix their brokenness also when you pull away. Will it ever come back together? Sometimes yes, oft times no, I do say unto you. Let me work it out I say unto you. Even I do speak on: not only in the romance department do I speak of, but in many categories of relationships. They are wide and varied such as wives, husbands, children, parents, co-workers, friends, associates of every kind. Of course, to some of these you will never depart from, but I speak emotionally you must move on until and unless I re-align the relationship the right way, when it goes wrong or sour. Never stay and argue, but allow Me to work whoever it is that there is conflict with. Seek to work it out, but if a person is not ready to listen, move on. Two can never walk closely together unless they be agreed. It is printed in the pages of My word and is truth.

Amos 3:3 "Can two walk together, except they be agreed?" Why am I teaching this My child and what do I mean little one? Why? For it is badly needed for My little ones get stuck and move not forward. Tell them bring their heart to Me, for I will surely mend their broken heart. What I do mean is for freedom to occur in My children. Many relationships will be healed in this hour, but I speak a strong warning to all My children. Fix, keep your eyes on Me only and concentrate on My great love, for we will surely walk closely together in this end time hour. A love affair do we have, for I am your husband and love you I do, My dear bride. Now I say on: abide in Me. All things are well and being worked out by My hand little ones. Breathe in Me new life and live close unto My heart. I will surely take you into my bosom and a sweetness like never before will you find if only you let Me. I have spoken and that is surely thus saith the Lord your God."

11-21-12 "Seasons Are Changing"

Hearing the Lord speak: "A **shift** I say unto all My children who have ears to hear has already taken place. It is spiritual ears I am talking about. Guard your hearts well, for I will reveal. You are coming into a new place in Me, many of you, I say and as such, the devil would seek to blind you and devour you. Know you not, right before the greatest victories, the heaviest battles are fought? Some fall and never get up. Guard your hearts I say again for many would seek to divert your attention from Me. The seasons change, I speak. Spring comes then summer, next fall and last winter. All have their place but I reveal much in this letter. We will start with spring. What are you hearing child, a refreshing? Yes but more than that. In the **spring time** the flowers bud and the birds sing their song. The birds are chirping along and every sound is refreshing unto your hearts. You come alive in Me, many of you during spring. Still springtime is just preparation for the full glory of summer. In **summer** the fullness of the warmth of spring is realized. Summer days are glorious are they not? Yet I speak on and say. The heat is hard to bare but yet I reveal many glorious truths about summer. In the summer time many of you relax and even take a vacation. It is a time of reveling in My wonders. The summers reveal a part of My very nature. I have you to be either hot or cold, not lukewarm, don't you know? Yet I say that in My word, but out of them both which you think is My choice for you? Of course to be on fire and be full of the heat of God. What did I mean when I put that in My word that way? **"Lukewarm will make you sick My children."** Now I take you to **fall**. Ahhh a time of changes of the leaves. Beauty all around you and cool brisk air. Fall is a time of refreshing again I say. After the heat I cool you off. Now comes the **winter** and the heavy cold. It will make you yearn to get to the spring. Why do I make all the four seasons? To show you **lives patterns**. Spring summer fall and winter. Every season is for a reason. Read in Ecclesiastes about where there is a season for everything and a time. Flourish in me. Each season of your life you may compare to the warm hot cool and cold of the year. **"Transition times I say unto you."** We will explore fall further. You are in the fall of the year are you not? Listen close My children for I will reveal a matter. Suffering afflictions have many of you been in. Now a new day has dawned and many of you are seeking to draw nigh unto Me. With the cost you have paid, comes the glory. It is pay day time. Arise and partake of My goodness. You are at a breakthrough. The seasons changed did they not? You have transitioned into a new day, I say again. Take the blinders off. You are here children, what have you been waiting for? Canaan land. **"Slay the giants partake of the land. True milk and honey are flowing."** Why ye hesitate? Many of you just have to just go ahead and cross over. Some are already in the land. The season has already changed. Wake up I do say again. Love affair I do have with My children. I am sweeter than the honeycomb. Be consumed with My great love. You'll never get enough of Me. You that seek the fullness, you will overflow to many others. Some have even already had to ask Me to stay My hand, for the glory was so bright. March forward and partake of the sweetness. **"I say unto you come and dine."** It is My voice that speaketh."

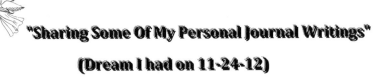

"Sharing Some Of My Personal Journal Writings"

(Dream I had on 11-24-12)

There was a giant with blonde hair, other people all around. I was out in a hall with people. The giant came and hit me on the arm. Then he and others started crowding and pushing into my home. The rest pushing in looked mentally challenged, but the giant was in front. Others were helping me push all of them out of my home, but I was mostly pushing the giant by myself. Finally we got them all out of the door. None was left getting into my home.

One interpretation: One person told me when the giant hit me; he was coming against my authority in the Lord. I realized in dreams that everything is not always from God, but feel this dream was significant. Also know in a dream there can be more than one interpretation at times, like a dual meaning.

Interpretation: This is what I heard the spirit of the Lord speak to me: "Take your shoes off, for you are standing on holy ground. That is what I say. Write it down. Once again we readdress an issue here. Your fort has been strong, yet there are times you have allowed others to sway you. Now you will remain strong in Me. The strongman most times is 'fear'. That is why he was bigger than the others. The enemy attacks the mind. That is why you seen the others as mentally challenged or so you thought. Satan and the spirits are evil.
(It came to me right now; we are not fighting a physical battle, but a spiritual. Our weapons are not carnal but mighty, in the pulling down of strongholds. Amen."

Ephesians 6: 10-18 No fear is in these last days. It is being broken off us, and we will march together in unison in God's army. Joel's army for sure.)

(12-18-12) "Journal Writings To Share, Cont."

Heard the Lord speak: "All over again, I hear your voice crying out. Like a candle in the wind? No, for I say a candle in the dark lighting up this world for Jesus, for Me. How can a candle in the dark talk or speak? I will reveal. The candle is Me inside of you. Is it a little or a big voice? According to how much you let Me speak is how bright it is. *If you are speaking I can't speak. If you are yielding totally to Me, words of pure life are pouring out."* Close it up, close it all up but hearing My voice sharper, clearer wherever you are at. I have spoken."

(1-12-13) "Journal Writings To Share, Cont."

I wept and wept as I heard this word and still do: "My peace I give unto you, not as the world giveth. They take everything back and leave you with sorrow. Read it now the **14th chapter of St. John**. I will bless you as never before. Begin and end with the love. It is the end, it is the beginning of all things for surely I so loved the world that I sent My Son, My only begotten Son into the world to redeem mankind. Do you think I do not love mankind? Think again My beloved, My daughter, for surely I do. *"I love the street people, the homeless, the wretched prostitutes, the con artists, the drunkards and the homosexuals. All of mankind, daughter do I love. The sin I detest, it is a stench in my very nostrils, but the sinner I adore!"* Think I died on the cruel cross in vain? Redeem them back to Me I do. They just need to look at the bloody sacrifice, My atonement for sins. *"Call on Me in the day of trouble and I shalt surely deliver thee and thou shalt glorify Me."* It has begun, a closer walk with Me than ever before. Deny yourself, pick up the cross daily and walk in My beloved footsteps. Journey has begun in earnest. Never has there been a day like today to seek My face. My end time army is marching and surely you are leading as many others. Refresh often in My presence, for that is your key. Your victory march will be sweeter for it daughter, My beloved, for I pour out My love on you this day. Want more? Surely I will give it. Now be My instrument and reach the people with it. The key is *praise* daughter in the face of all adversity. I will see you through all things beloved. I have spoken."

2-13-13 "Sin Is Dividing The Nation"

"Sin is dividing the nation. I am hearing the Lord say further: yeah My people, get off the stool of do nothing and the back burner and live. Many of you are still hesitating to step out, when I say it is time to move further up into My kingdom. Learn of Me, My little ones and of My ways. Gird on new strength for a mystery will be revealed. What is this mystery? The mystery of iniquity that doth already work I say unto your heart. Divide not the camp of the holy ones. You're wondering what that is about? I will reveal. In your hearts many of you do not seek Me in the fullness. Error has slipped in. Cautioning you I am. You divide and spoil your own people. You mark them of I am with this group, you are of that group. I'll have it not My beloved children, for many of you walk in error. Repent of your evil deeds, for do you think it not evil to bring division? Enemy lines are drawn, but why would you fight each other My children? While some would say I am of Paul and others I am of Apollos, you are losing the meaning of it all. It is all about getting on the same page and fighting the good fight of faith. To each his own is not in the least bit, I say unto you. The truth is, I have a united front. Do you not know little ones, that I have a church; one who will stand the test of time? I speak on and bring clarity and My servant doth hear the sound of My voice. Judge the word, for I would have you to do so, for it is of Me and a heavy word I do speak this day. ***"Try the spirits and know it is of Me, My little ones of a surety."*** Guard your hearts, for many of you are listening to strange voices, I do say unto you. Let not anyone into the secret place of your hearts without My direct permission. Go there daughter, for it is Me that is writing this word and not you. You are only a willing vessel, but many times you just as soon, not deliver My word, but deliver it you must, for many need to hear it and act upon it. In the affairs of the heart, I speak again through this servant as in times before. The enemy would try to get you off focus, off track. If I put it together then that is well, fine and good. If not, I say unto you leave it alone. Proof is in the pudding. If I do bring it together, it will be a sweet love song and grand music will you play and sing together. The union will bring glory to My name and that is what it is all about; not yourselves and having your own way. ***"Seek My face and I will give you the*** *desires of your heart."* Still I say on: in these last hours, time is closing up as you do know it. Many do not have the mark of true discipleship and do you think I have you linked up with them? Think again. They will rend you every time and bring you heart ache and much pain and sorrow, I do say unto you. Truly I ask you little ones, how that two can walk together unless they be agreed? They can't and I send you strong warnings My children, My people. Get out while you still can, for the error is slipping in deeper and deeper and many of you know it not. The ones not crucifying their flesh will take you down a long, hard road. Make up your minds to who this does apply, for this is a turning, pivotal point for some. I have spoken. Many of you surely need to get this settled before you wind up with someone of a baser sort. My beloveds, I speak peace unto your hearts. The enemy is out for war and destruction. You are the apple of My eye and surely I do rebuke those that I love and chasten. Guard your hearts little ones, for out of it proceeds the issues of life. I have spoken."

8-5-12 "Sing A Little Or A Big Song"

Thus saith the Lord: "Well people, let's open it up, the great title of what I give you tonight. Is it profound? Do you like the little, the simple, or do you look for a big thing like Naaman to do? What about a song? Much in every way, I prepare My people for the days ahead. Dark and stormy on every hand. War in the land. Believe you not Me? I have warned My people time and time again, but yet many of you believe it not. Now what? Trouble's ahead, how you going to get through it? By My Spirit leading you through it. Now guide Me you say and I am through simplicity. Keep it simple. Sing a new song in your heart, for that is for your joy. Keep it simple I say, but yet you complicate it. Why do you do that? Guard your heart, for out of it proceeds the issues of life. Love simplicity and not offenses. So many of My children hold on to a grudge. How are you going to sing when you hold a grudge or ought against your brother? Let it be established. It is gonna rain. Gonna? This is important here that My children understand. My language is established in My kingdom. You come along and slaughter it. Do I laugh? Do I cry? I smile. Being such, I tell you why. Many of you have thought your God was a God of no understanding. I identify with your emotions, feelings and all you go through. A heart of compassion have I and I listen for your hearts cry. I have you find humor in some situations and lighten up. My yoke is easy and my burden is light. **Mat. 11:28-29** "I give you scriptures to back everything up. I speak the truth. I lie not. Still, I wink not at sin and know this day that it is forever settled in heaven's courts. I have all to repent and to be righteous. Now let's move on. Go tell the people, I am coming back soon. As such, every one of you who name My name ought to be rejoicing, but warning others. Warning them about what? My second coming draweth nigh. It is not out there somewhere, it is nigh even at your door. The trumpets are blowing, hear them not? One final is yet to come and then the end. Blast, I will split the eastern sky wide open and come again. Believe My report? It is all in the word, yet going back; I say it is going to rain. What is that about? Holy Ghost rain falling on you now. It is the unction of my spirit falling and being felt upon my people now, upon their heads. *"Meaning you are in revival and the fires are stirred, you learned. "* The simple will take this message to their heart; the unlearned will throw it away. Be comfortable among yourselves and love one another. Give not place to the enemy, for he delights in division. Slay the dragon, confound the enemy and that is thus saith the Lord. What is that about? Holy Ghost rain falling on you now. It is the unction of My Spirit falling, being felt upon My people now, upon their heads. Meaning, you are in revival and the fires are stirred you learned. How do you do that? By staying in this word, reading, devouring it and pretending not to be a Christian, but being one. Love simplicity again do I say. Take Me to the bank, deposit love and see want you get back? A heart of love for your fellow man and a song. I have you love one another, guard each other's back. Yes child you are each other's keepers. Sing a new song unto Me. It is one of the ages. Now, what I say is this; simply to love simplicity honor Me and be done with it. Quit trying to complicate the simple My children. It is all I am posting this night through this servant."

9-5-12 "Slay The Giants"

Thus saith the Lord: "A new day has dawned and as I told you before children, you are entering into a different season. Yet I warn you beforehand. Even though there are still giants in the land, I am removing them. What does it take? It takes the full armor of God. Stir and shake your faith up, My children. What instrument did it take for David My servant to be able to defeat Goliath, the giant of Gath? It took a small slingshot and five smooth stones out of a brook. What then? He had his weapons in his hands and he used them for my glory and defeated the tormenter of Israel. It always takes obedience and I use the things at hand for you to overcome. Read My word in the book of revelation. It says you overcome by the blood of the Lamb and the word of your testimony. Be faithful, be true until the end. Hear the sound of My voice and live. It is a day like no other. I am that I am and I right all the wrongs in your life. I am restoring what the devil has stolen from you and repairing the breach. Give not place to the flesh but partake of Me only. If I say move, move and if I say stop, stop. I know the enemy territory and I go before you and warn you of the pitfalls. Shoot straight My children, for the enemy you fight is the devil and his unholy angels. Destroy the devil's works by declaring righteousness everywhere you go. Have no mercy ever on devil spirits, for they are from hell and will try to get you to believe them. Listen not and allow them not to talk, but proclaim unto them My holy word. The finger of God it will take to remove them. Be instant in season and out of season. Never look back My children. Remember Lot's wife. Love you I do. I say unto you, love the people who are possessed by evil spirits and judge them not, but deliver them only when they are truly crying out and ready. It is by My grace you stand and are not consumed yourselves. Keep on the firing line and I will show you when it is time to come apart and rest. Some err by getting out of the battle and that is good at times, but yet they give place and back off the fight. There is always a time to refresh when weary, but when I say you need to get back in the fight, move quickly to obey Me. Know ye not it is Me that is keeping you and I will stand beside you always? Deliver My people you leaders, for many are hurting. Use the sword, the word of God and I will bless you as never before. Fare ye well and again, I speak that I love you. My beloved children are the apple of My eye. Never give up, but look thou unto Me and I will deliver and see you through. A great refreshing is on the way for many. Still many of you are not paying the cost. Make up your minds to go all the way and you will never regret it My children."

11-9-12 "Strengthened You Are Becoming"

Hearing the Lord speak: "Denominational walls are coming down My children. It has gone on too long and I am stirring up the nests with many. I am getting you out of your comfort zones. Denominational tags have brought only division in My churches. Yet there be only one true church. The church of the living God. Which church is right and which is wrong you may ask? ***"Anyone of them that goes contrary to My word is surely wrong and whoever proclaims My word without compromise is right. It is that simple."*** I have a standard and I will always cause you to lift that standard up. It is a blood stained banner that I have you to lift up. The cost of your salvation was a bloody one My children. Did you not know also it has been a blood bath for many of My children who have been martyred for the cause of Christ? March on, for as I have told you in times past, a new day is dawning. Much pain and sorrow have many of you been through. Trouble is in the land and I am executing judgement throughout. ***"Still, there has always been a remnant, a chosen people preserved through the trials."*** Many of you shall walk in shoes that you have never walked in before. They are bigger shoes. You are filling them up walking in My steps. An angry God is pouring out

wrath, yet on My beloved, My chosen, My faithful ones, I am
raining down My glory bricks. I speak blessings unto you and
favor like you have never known in My courts. A glory train is
filling up. I have you to be on it. Did I say a new day is dawning? I
repeat it here yet again. A new day is dawning and with it
obstacles shall be overcome. The anointing is getting stronger
upon many of you and My glory is shining through. Peace in the
valley can be yours if only you pay the cost. The cost is great for
it is total surrender of everything. Lay it all on the altar, My
children. You need overcoming faith My children, to make it
through. The ones who have tapped into My hidden manna,
know what I mean. When you find Me in the secret place, you
will never want for another. You will find Me sweeter than
honey. I speak on: The journey is long and the enemy has fought
many of you. You have thought you could not take even one
more pain, one more heartache. Do you not know why My
beloved children? Satan wants to weaken you, to destroy you, for
he hates everything I love. It is My strength I have you to walk in.
Quit trying to figure it out and just abide in Me. Everything is
about to change. Be prepared and you can only do that by
looking unto Me. When you see the power of the holy people
scattered, know I am about to come on the scene like never
before. I am sweeping house and with all the great cleansing I am
doing and about to do in the land, there is an awakening like
never before. Revival is yours if you want it. Get in the flow, look
unto Me, for many miracles will you see as the end draweth nigh.
Look up, look up, look up, for you will find Me there. You have
looked down to the ground for too long. Angelic visitations are
being felt even stronger than before. Be aware that they are
visiting for a reason. They are strengthening and helping you.
Many shall see and converse with them. Stay humble, for the
devil would desire to lift you up with pride. With the new day
dawning there will be many opportunities to work in My
kingdom. Rule and govern with kindness, but with strength. I am
talking in large part to My leaders, for I have you to have ears to
hear and eyes to see. You must partake of Me, all of Me to be
effective. I close this love letter with an admonition. The troops
are marching in. When you are so weary you can't make it,

remember I have already walked this journey. Don't forget to refresh in My presence My children. The enemy would desire to turn you around in this late stage of the game. Draw nigh unto Me for I will surely refresh your very soul. Love you I do."

12-22-12 "The Anchor Holds-Get On Board"

Hearing the Lord say: "I speak again unto your heart as in times past. Surely I am visiting this particular nation for their sins. America rose up against Me and is suffering for her wrong doings. I speak on and I will reveal many things children. My chosen elect hear My voice and follow only Me. Winds may howl and winds may blow, but surely are you sheltered under My wing. Daughter, reveal what I say unto your heart and falter not, for the people need to hear this word. Though it is hard in places, I soften it up where it needs to be. I have chosen many of you, but yet there has been rebellion in the camp. Some of you have not continued on to follow Me in the fullness and I am not pleased. Did you not know that I said unto your hearts to hang on for the storms will get rougher? While many of you are debating whether to celebrate Christmas or not, the world is going to hell in a hand basket. Satan desires for you to lose your focus and will get you off track. Does that cover all? No I say it is many things more. Many of your hearts are no longer steadfast in Me, for you have drawn back. My fire is falling on this nation and I am separating the wheat from the chaff. You must not take your eyes off Me for even a minute, for satan will try to devour you. Did you not know many strong have fallen, giving place to the sins of the flesh? It starts with a little and goes from there. Seek not to follow the world and its cravings. Many of you are having a food battle and I am seeking to bring you into a place of perfect submission. Fasting will begin for many of you afresh, for it is time. Only listen to the sound of My voice. When I say fast and withhold, give not place to the flesh. It is strong and has its own voice. Just as I am getting you ready for longer and longer fasts, this word is going out to many who need to hear the sound of My voice on this matter also daughter. It is I who will give you the strength to withhold, but you have to seek Me, persevere I say unto you all. What was the message that has stuck with you for many a year daughter, from your own pastor? 'Shut up flesh!' Think I not give the man the message for this hour? ***"You must not yield to the flesh for it is constantly battling the spirit. They are at enmity, odds with one another. You will feed one and starve another."*** Now we go on to another subject matter. Restoring the years the locusts have stolen. Now how is that? I can replace mourning for joy, gladness for sorrow and laughter instead of crying. Get in the way that is how I say unto your hearts. The gospel expressway for all aboard, I do say unto you. I am visiting. Can't have it both ways daughter, as you do know and neither can they. Time to choose the greater and most needful part, My little ones. Choose Me, My ways to sup with Me in a hidden secret place. You know that place quite well, as do many of My chosen elect this goes to. I am more beautiful than the greatest picture ever painted on canvas. More fragrant than the most fragrant aromas in a flower. When you pick Me, you have found the lily in the valley and the pearl of great price. All aboard, get on the ship, for I am sailing this ship safely to harbor. It is the old ship of Zion I say. Its hull may be bent and battered, but this vessel sails on and the anchor surely holds. I will deliver it safely to port. I have spoken."

9-24-12 "The Ark- The Mark- Spiritual Israel"

Thus saith the Lord: "I will reveal further about many matters, My children. Some have sought after deeper truth and deeper truth shall they have. The Ark of the Covenant is being revealed tonight to many. It is a mystery and I will open it up. The bottom line as man says is now exposed. What I mean? I am bringing things to light and as I do, you will never wonder again. Still some will doubt this word but as always tell them to try the spirits daughter and see if it be so. I have no error, step in, but many would wonder and it is always right to seek My face before believing what anyone speaks. ***"The false will always tell you to take what they say and run with it. They seek their own glory and have you to look toward them and not Me."*** The true every time will point you to Jesus and desire you to know the words that come from above and not from them. You will not be deceived if you walk close enough to Me. Do not waver, as deception and false anti-christs are in the land. It is a spirit of unbelief touching the people I say.

"The Ark of the Covenant has never left my children." I explain further: it does not have to come back from anywhere, as that would mean it had to leave. My word was enthroned in the ark. It went before the mighty kings and the people to battle. I have protected My word from all generations. I perform My words. My very breath is life. I breathe into the very nostrils of man his first breath. The same with the spiritual. I speak and breathe life into My words. What I speak I back up or perform them. Your God cannot lie and you can take to the bank, My promises for they are yeah and amen. What else will we go into this night? My mark is 777, which I tell you before. You want to know more of it? Some I say again are seeking to go further in Me.

Did I not say in My word to seek and ye shall find? Ponder no more for it is My heart to reveal hidden mysteries to My chosen elect. All will not hear this message, but some will. It is the ones with spiritual ears and eyes that see. It is truth that I speak of. Seven is a number. It is the fullness, the message of hope, the heavenly number. I am that I am. You want to go further in Me children, you can. How will this number operate some are wondering? Will you literally wear it? Yes and no. Wake up, wake up, wake up I say again and again. Take the blinders off and live. ***"Seven is My perfect number, the number of completion if you please."*** Get full in Me, wear My number and worry not about a literal implanting of it in your forehead or hands. It is already implanted on many of you. You are sealed, you are marked and I say in a spiritual sense, it is literally upon some of you already. This child has My mark upon her forehead. Quit looking for the natural and believe more and more shall be added. Want the spiritual? Carnal interpretations shall never work. Now we go to the conclusion. You get weary of My words some of you? Why do you not get weary listening to long reports of satan's lies? All are not weary yet I know the ones who hesitate to take Me on in the fullness. Many put too much stock in flesh and blood Israel. Are they My beloved? Yes they are, yet many more are my beloved also. Time for the blinders to come off. This sister knows the cost of this word, but still she will obey Me for this needs to be spoken. Many err in their thinking and their judgement.

I love Israel surely I do, but yet I speak on. I came to My own and they received Me not. Yet I visit them again and again to wake them up. That never changes My love. Still I love all nations, all kindred's and all tribes. I died for the sins of the whole world, not part. Bleeding suffering Jesus on the cross was your way back to God. Don't you understand yet My children? Those of the perfect seed are in Isaac. Know ye not what it says in **Romans Chapter 9**? It would pay you all to study this chapter and learn. Read **verse 25** closely. "<u>As he saith also in o'see, I will call them my people, which were not my people; and her beloved, which was not beloved.</u>" My church is blood bought with a price and I delight in all My chosen ones. Love Israel, look to her and the scriptures. In the end times such as now she will reveal much to you about My coming. It is a time bomb ready to explode I say over there. Still I say she is blinded till this day and her eyes need opening. Some over there are seeing and many more shall have their eyes open.

Pray for her and the peace of Jerusalem surely. Still I receive all who call on me in truth and in spirit. In the end times, the mighty revival sweeping the land will come from all nations. My bride has to make herself ready. Array yourself in white and take your stand for righteousness. Love you I do. Fare ye well."

8-6-12 "The Awakening Is Upon You"

Thus saith the Lord: "Pay the cost. Know you not it was for you I died on Calvary's cross? What do I want of you? Obedience in the highest order. When I call you out of slumber awake. That is My command unto you. Do you not think your God that formed you in your mother's womb longs for your perfect obedience? I am the God from heaven that thunders. In My presence there is peace and joy. Abide in Me. Yield unto Me and live to the fullest. Many of you have been having battles that are almost unbearable. Some have lost loved ones that have left holes in your heart. Many also have had broken relationships in their marriages. The affairs of the heart hurt badly. It is worse than any cut that there is. It is time for restoration and I am the God who is coming on the scene to heal the brokenness. Much of you have hurt, but much I restore unto you. In the end times you shall rejoice in a way you thought not possible. You shall cry out to Me and you shall see the things fixed deemed impossible to man. I am the restorer of the breach. To some I am putting back homes that have been wrecked by putting other things first. I am breaking disobedience off families. I will cause the heart of the child to turn back to the father and the heart of the father to the child. Be at peace with one another and quit squabbling. I break discord off you if only you yield unto Me. You can walk with one another in perfect harmony. I am soon to bring a millennium age in at my appearing. It is getting closer and closer. ***The lion and the lamb shall lie down together and you shall study war no more.*** My children look up, for your redemption draweth nigh. Now is the time to come closer unto Me. Look not to the right or the left but look straight ahead, for that is where I am."

3-10-16 "The Bride"

Heard this beautiful word spoken and I felt the Lord's heart for us. He truly sees us in the beloved. Tears, He is so wonderful! "Time stood still in My courts the day I married you, My beautiful bride. I lifted the veil at Calvary and saw you as you were, chaste, a virgin. I saw no fault or blemish in My beloved, the church. There will never be another you, unique with many abilities.

You are one My church, My beloved bride."

8-7-12 "The End Times"

The word of the Lord: "For I would say unto you My child, preach on for I am coming soon. Many are the afflictions the righteous shall suffer, yet I will deliver them out of all. In truth and in spirit have you come and I will reveal further. Thus saith the Lord: My people are destroyed for lack of knowledge. In ignorance do they seek Me their way. I call them forth in Jesus' name. It is an end time army I am raising up. Their thoughts, their ways will I destroy for I am tired of it. Tried and true have you been to Me. My servant you are and I call you blessed. Peace abideth on your house for you come to Me for all answers. It will be a short work I will do and will cut it off in righteousness. Never mind what others may think of you, for I love you. My child, sweetness is in your nature and you don't even like to think it, but it is Me that placed it there. Enemy lines are drawn and I am crossing over. My people are tired, weary, and need a fresh anointing and I am bringing it to them. Yes, many calamities shall fall, yet I abide faithful. To Me you will always come for answers. Many of your friends are seeking Me also, for it is the last days and hungry have they become. Purify My people. Child, do you not see? My word is pure. When you preach and proclaim it you are setting the captives free. The anointing is upon you for I placed it there. In trials and tribulations must you go through with your brothers and sisters. Yet I never fail. I know not how to fail. Publish My word, for I will back it up. You speak of Me. Those that know My voice hear you well. Tell My people I love them and will return for them soon; tenderly I write."

6-13-12 "The False Revealed"

"I speak unto you this day My child, to beware of the ***hooded man***. What would I mean by this? Some would speak of a gospel without hope and even call themselves your friend. I reveal all. ***"Be careful and guard against false prophets and discern their voice."*** How will you know the difference? I reveal truth and not error. The world paints a false picture. At the end of the rainbow is always a promise. I rebuke and chasten My children, but I never leave them without hope. It is the world system that leaves them high and dry without a savior. When I reveal My great wrath to come, I also reveal My great mercy to the obedient who pull out of the world system. Keep your distance from the false My children. I set you free. Be not entangled again with the bondage of the world and its ways. Many are scared to even sing a happy song. The grim reaper has even robbed them of the joy of the innocent things in life. I reveal when a thing is wrong. I have you not walk in sin. I have you be free and delight in Me. Have you ever felt light My children? That is only when I have removed the bondages of the world off your back. Go before Me and tell My people I am coming back soon, but also tell them I keep coming back and they are not ready. What do I mean? The people are ashamed of Me and seek another God to serve. They serve Baal and Baal shall rend them in the end. He is the false anti-christ system and will be revealed every time. What is his measure? Weights and balances and he is found wanting. Be ashamed of your judgements My people for many of you try to put restrictions on your fellow man. Love within the confounds of My grace. Sure I give you barriers, but I break the walls of divisions off My children. Rule books are thrown away in My kingdom. Never be lax but walk with Me, seeking My face and you will know the truth from the error. Why? I am truth and My children who hear My voice truly delight in Me. Keep your balance, but love deep in all you do. I am a God of love and grace and I have you enjoy the beauties of life. Still I warn you not to be carried away with great wealth and gold. If you have it, use it for My glory and kingdom but strive not after it. I have My children prosper and be in peace. All the gold in the world can never satisfy your soul. Only I can fill the longing within you. Know ye not this day I desire a people after My own heart? Be righteous even as I am righteous. Crave Me and I shall give you the desires of your heart. Keep your balance in all things. ***"Beware of the*** *false sound."* Learn to discern in all things. Keep your distance from the ones who would pull you down. Fare ye well and keep on loving Me, for I tenderly talk to My children. All who will hear the sound of My voice I reward. True and righteous are My judgements."

6-11-12 "The Fruits Of The Spirit"

Thus saith the Lord: "I am just and I have you walk in freedom. Study it out. **Galatians 5:22** "But the fruit of the spirit is love, joy, peace, longsuffering, gentleness, goodness, faith, **23** meekness, temperance: against such there is no law. **24** and they that are Christ's have crucified the flesh with the affections and lusts. **25** if we live in the spirit, let us also walk in the spirit." What do you see here? *Nine fruits?* I give you more understanding. All are fruits of righteousness. Take them apart. (1) **Love**- this fruit imparted is a joy walk for when you have this fruit you shall move on. Where to? (2) **Joy**- because they go together. Love conquers all and is next of kin to joy. Believe My report my people. Guide me in truth you say? Then study My word. Love and joy intermingled with peace brings great victory. (3)**Peace**- of the soul to lie down in the battle and rest completely in Me. How do you get that peace that passeth all understanding? Gird on your loins and search it out. I do all things new. When you turn to Me, the gift of righteousness is yours. I restore your soul. All your understanding is encompassed in four words- love, joy, peace and longsuffering which brings you to the next level of victory. (4)**Longsuffering**- is to do good to all people even when they despitefully use you and cast out your name for evil. I reveal further: March on, for your battle is hot, but I bring you relief My people to study My word and know My great truths. Reach out for more.

(5)**Gentleness**- ahh... My children, I make you gentle for when you suffer awhile, I establish you.

(6)**Goodness**- is another tool and weapon you may use for the kingdom of God. For it is pure and full of truth. I bring goodness into your nature. I reveal more for when you love Me and serve Me; I partake of your nature you partake of Mine. Meaning? *"We walk in truth together."*
Mercy is poured out all over you and new heights you keep climbing. Understand now? I reveal further. ***Walk in truth but walk in love.*** Reach out for more always for you can always draw nigh and come closer.

(7)**Faith**- is another key and level you shall obtain. Walk in the door, take the key and open yourselves wide open to the mysteries of the kingdom. What are they? Truth, mercy and righteousness; believing when all the world says you are a hypocrite or a liar. Know ye not the sound of My voice? Reach higher. Faith walk is an end time ministry in itself. All My children should walk in faith believing what I say. All true Christians walk in faith and not doubt. Believe, My people. A special mark is put on the prophets of this day. They will always seek to guide and lead you in paths of righteousness. They will promote not themselves, but others and esteem them higher. They will call on you to believe, to honor the prophets of old and receive the whole word. It is a faith walk all the way. Look at Abraham. Believe not my promise to him? See that I did perform My word to him. A mighty calling have some of you and I am moving you forward. ***"Get out of the stagnation of spirit. Move forward."***

(9)**Temperance**- get converted. Love simplicity and honor Me. What do you mean? Temperance is longsuffering in the reverse. It is putting on withholding being moderate in all things. When you are at this level you have overcome many things of the flesh. Why did I not say all? ***"You walk in fullness to get it all."*** In the flesh you shall reap corruption, but in the spirit you shall overcome. Now do you understand? There is more always more. You say I left out one. I have not. I saved it to last to put it all together.

(8)**Meekness**- you have to get it first before you can move to temperance. Why? They go together one at a time building on one another. When you are meek you won't know it but others shall. Know ye not the meek shall inherit the earth? *"It is being in My presence that brings meekness and makes you fit for the Master's use. "*

All things come together. I will supply. I will supply well. Trust Me, My people for I will perform all I said I would in your hearts and lives. Now build them together. All the stumbling blocks? No the *"stepping stones."*

I will conclude the matter of the 'fruits of the spirit.' I will reveal 'lust of the flesh' another day and that is thus saith the Lord." (Still waiting for the Lord to reveal on the lust of the flesh.)

1-21-13 "The Mark Of The Beast Is Coming Is Here"

Hearing the Lord speak: "The mark of the beast is coming get ready, get prepared. For yeah I would speak further My children, it is already here. Great mercy and great truth is being revealed, for I have My people prepared and warned. The rider on the pale horse is riding as I told you before. He is death and with him he brings a mark, a stamp. Yeah he brings a spiritual mark before the physical one. Buyer beware, I say unto you again and again for truly you cannot buy or sell without his stamp, his image. Will you be here? Wake up, My people, wake up I say again, for it is here and it is now. It will be upon your forehead or in your hand as the holy word says. Take it not. While the world is carrying you away with easy believism and falsehood, he has snuck in on many of you. Can you make it through you may ask? Is your Lord's hand shortened that he cannot feed a multitude with a few loaves of bread and a few fishes? Think again little ones. *"The same God of old is supplying all your needs according to His riches in glory."* Get on board for the long haul little ones. I do call you little ones time and again. In My eyes you are My beloved the apple of My eye. My church is slumbering. Wake her up, the bride of Christ. She is Mine and I have her adorn herself with My attire. She is lacking, but when I come back, she will be on fire and nothing lacking for her heart will only desire Me and that in the fullness. Get aboard the gospel ship, for it is sailing to the ports of glory. Receive not the wicked ones image or his design upon you little ones. ***In truth and in spirit you must walk or you will be deceived.*** " Give not place to man and what he tells, bids you do. If it goes against the grain of what I am speaking, have it not, I say unto you and simply toss it aside. Careless daughters and sons are some of you. You are too slack and I am having you tighten up the belt. The truth is the ***Babylonian kingdom*** is still standing. Know it not? Destroy it, the yoke off your backs. How? Turn to Me with your everything. Let Me take control and consume you with My love. The fullness has come. Which do you want? Do you want My fullness consuming your very being or do you want the fullness with pride? I speak on. Mark your days on earth for they are numbered. Man's days are few and truly marked with sorrow and trouble. I am soon to create a new heaven and a new earth for I do all things well and on time. First, I set up My millennium kingdom, for My children shall reign with Me a thousand years. Let it go, let it all go. The discord within your hearts for your brethren. Prove Me, turn all things over in My hands and leave the cares of the world alone. Forgive easily; forgive quickly, lest satan should get an advantage over you. I speak farewell and peace unto your hearts. Quit studying and start praying and that is thus saith the Lord your God. I have spoken."

Note: To clarify when the Lord spoke 'studying' in the last line, it was not referring to studying the 'word'. This was our studying and trying to figure things out with a carnal understanding.

9-26-12 "The Pale Horseman Is Riding"

The Lord speaks this day: "What is going on My children? The battle is getting harder. As of late many have wanted to throw in the towel. I say, do it not, for I explain more to your understanding. The reason the battle is fiercer is satan knows his days are numbered. He is taking peace from the earth. He rides upon the **pale horse.** The pale horse is death. As he sits upon it, confusion and strife is magnifying everywhere. Did not I tell you before that this is a time in history like never before My children? I am preparing you for the days that are ahead. Beware of the rider upon the pale horse, for he sets out to deceive you and take your life.

We will explore a matter. Look carefully at **Revelation 6:7-8**. What does it say My people?

<u>"And when he had opened the fourth seal, I heard the voice of the fourth beast say, come and see. And I looked, and behold a pale horse: and his name that set on him was death, and hell followed with him. And power was given unto them over the fourth part of the earth, to kill with sword, and with hunger, and with death, and with the beasts of the earth."</u>

Remove the blinders, for great truth is soon to be revealed. The enemy in the land is not deceitful without a reason... His reason is clear... He wants to swallow you up. He uses people and many times the closest of friends and family. The pain is deeper than when a stranger comes against you. He wants you to throw in the towel as I mentioned earlier. That is his deception... His game if you please. If the ones who usually believe in you and stick close to your side suddenly depart, it is a heavier blow. Things will be going smoothly and he will blind sight you with attacks you are not expecting. What do you see in the two verses above? Is it the plagues being poured out? Surely, but more than that I tell you. Not only is the enemy visiting with plagues, so am I. What do I mean? *I use satan for My own purpose.* He is evil he is destructive, but yet I allow him to destroy. The reason is My anger is kindled against this nation. To all the nations that forget God, the Sovereign One, I will visit and turn them into hell. I play not. Still there is a **remnant.** There is always a remnant of believers. Do you not see My children, there just is one power and it is of God? He is the deceiver and his is a limited power. *"I have all power... 'All' I say again."* Satan only can tap in to what I allow. Do you remember the fierce wind I rebuked that was blowing on the seas recorded in My word? Satan had it blowing... I calmed the wind and the storm. Even the winds and the sea must listen to the sound of My voice. In these last days I give you a warning. You must be in obedience to make it through. There is no other way My children. Satan roars and it is time to get all the way into the boat. Get on board for your captain knows how to steer this vessel."

7-29-2000 "The Second Coming Is Upon You- And You Know It Not"

Rev. 6:12 "And I beheld when he had opened the sixth seal, and, lo, there was a great earthquake; and the sun became black as sackcloth of hair, and the moon became as blood;
Rev. 17:6 "And I saw the woman drunken with the blood of the saints, and with the blood of the martyrs of Jesus: and when I saw her, I wondered with great admiration. The Lord speaks: *"The moon is blood is what I said."* What do I mean? The saints have been martyred already. The moon is the light. When is it the light? Of the night. *"The light of the world is Me. I am shining through darkness. The darkness is here now."* I speak further My children: As blood and be blood are one and the same. I will explain so there is no confusion. My words are always clear and simple. In the beginning was Me. I have always been. Which way are you going? To the end? Maybe you are starting at the first. Ahhh I got you... Words written by Me have always a *flow.* All creation is crying out in travail. I speak on. You think not the sixth seal been opened already? Think again. The horsemen are already riding; don't you know My beloved children? Time will be no more shortly. You are already at the end and many of you know it not. *"Open your eyes look up and see Me in the clouds of glory."* The signs are surely in the sky and in all creation. The moon as blood you don't see? See it spiritual first. Will it be a literal? Wait for I will reveal. First you have to have the spiritual before you can have the literal. Some things in My word are literal, some figuratively. Will the moon I created actually turn to blood literally? Yes and no. It was symbolic yet the answer lies above. *"The devil is drunk on the blood of the saints I say again."* He is ruling in his hateful

kingdom with an iron rod of pride. Some of My children are still taking part of his Babylonian empire. Come out now I say and partake only of the heavenly kingdom. The second coming is upon you. Don't you see child? The light is come. *"The devil has been drunk on the blood of the saints for all time. My saints have already been martyred. That is the revelation."*

The second coming is now not out there somewhere. I am coming back now for My people. My bride is being made ready. Ready for what? The Marriage Supper of the Lamb. When is that? When the people see I have already come for them and they were not ready. That is why I am delaying my coming. My word is true. That is why I am pouring out My Spirit in these last days. To wake them up. Then I will come. It will be a mighty shaking! I shake the people, I revive My people.

The marriage supper of the Lamb: **Rev. 19: 1** "And after these things I heard a great voice of much people in heaven, saying, alleluia; salvation, and glory, and honour, and power, unto the Lord our God:

2 for true and righteous are his judgments: for he hath judged the great whore, which did corrupt the earth with her fornication, and hath avenged the blood of his servants at her hand.

3 and again they said, alleluia and her smoke rose up for ever and ever.

4 and the four and twenty elders and the four beasts fell down and worshipped God that sat on the throne, saying, amen; alleluia.

5 and a voice came out of the throne, saying, praise our God, all ye His servants, and ye that fear him, both small and great.

6 and I heard as it were the voice of a great multitude, and as the voice of many waters, and as the voice of mighty thunderings, saying, alleluia: for the Lord God omnipotent reigneth.

7 let us be glad and rejoice, and give honour to Him: for the marriage of the Lamb is come, and His wife hath made herself ready.

8 and to her was granted that she should be arrayed in fine linen, clean and white: for the fine linen is the righteousness of saints.

9 and he saith unto me, write, blessed are they which are called unto the Marriage Supper of the Lamb. And he saith unto me, these are the true sayings of God.

10 and I fell at his feet to worship him. And he said unto me, see thou do it not: I am thy fellowservant, and of thy brethren that have the testimony of Jesus: worship God: for the testimony of Jesus is the Spirit of prophecy.

11 and I saw heaven opened, and behold a white horse; and He that sat upon him was called faithful and true, and in righteousness He doth judge and make war.

12 His eyes were as a flame of fire, and on His head were many crowns; and He had a name written, that no man knew, but He Himself.

13 and He was clothed with a vesture dipped in blood: and His name is called the Word of God.

14 and the armies which were in heaven followed Him upon white horses, clothed in fine linen, white and clean.

15 and out of His mouth goeth a sharp sword, that with it He should smite the nations: and He shall rule them with a rod of iron: and He treadeth the winepress of the fierceness and wrath of Almighty God.

16 and He hath on His vesture and on His thigh a name written, King of Kings, and Lord of Lords.

17 and I saw an angel standing in the sun; and he cried with a loud voice, saying to all the fowls that fly in the midst of heaven, come and gather yourselves together unto the supper of the great God;

18 that ye may eat the flesh of kings, and the flesh of captains, and the flesh of mighty men, and the flesh of horses, and of them that sit on them, and the flesh of all men, both free and bond, both small and great.

19 and I saw the beast, and the kings of the earth, and their armies, gathered together to make war against Him that sat on the horse, and against His army.

20 and the beast was taken, and with him the false prophet that wrought miracles before him, with which he deceived them that had received the mark of the beast, and them that worshipped his image. These both were cast alive into a lake of fire burning with brimstone.

21 and the remnant were slain with the sword of him that sat upon the horse, which sword proceeded out of his mouth: and all the fowls were filled with their flesh."

6-22-12 "The Time Has Come"

Thus saith the Lord: "Press on for more details of the soon coming king of kings. I come riding on a white horse. In righteousness do I appear fully clothed. Your battles will then be over. It is of Me I speak further to you My children of this sister. You will receive My words. What is it that keeps you from drawing closer? Get rid of it, for no idol would I have you put before My face. Tell on. The days of wine and roses are over. What do I mean? Wining and dining with the world. You think I am pleased with your harlotry? You think I do not see? I see everything. I know everyone. Think this is a sharp word? I have sharper. They will come under subjection to Me or be cut asunder. Many of the times have I called you closer. Many are the times you resisted. I no longer wink at sin. Come closer, I will reveal more. You have hurt My heart with your much words of complaining. How you say when you speak it not aloud? I hear the thoughts. They are loud and clear. Come after Me, My people, I will reveal more. Steady on your feet are many of you tried and true. Still to others I talk with sharpness. Trust not your own self for flesh is weak. I warn you time and again yet ye think you have it all figured out. What? How to operate in the flesh and in the spirit realm? You cannot for one must die. This child stopped here to repent, because she thought she ate too much at lunch, but she did not. An extra drumstick, I allow her. She knows what I am talking about. She is laughing now. *"Lighten up my people."* Now you wonder if I wrote this or not? Try the spirits you will see. You see, after repentance comes, your burden is lifted. What do I mean? You carry a heavy yoke many of you. I have you light. Be patient. Tell the people I am coming back for a blood washed church, joyous and of great report. What do I mean? Your testimony is important children. Can you all come a little closer to Me children? Ahh now you can. I love My children, I speak tenderly, yet many times I have to rebuke as a father does his children. Why? I love each one. You are all in My kingdom, I write to you, but I have you bring many more in. Trust Me for more child. I am not through. What is of the great tribulation? When will it be? It is now. You are in the beginning of it and you know it not. The world has you deceived, many of you. Yet I reveal. I am coming back for a healthy church, one that has washed their self clean in the ***blood of the Lamb. "Yes child, I give hope at the end. I never leave My people without hope."*** Many are ready. Many will not be ready as much as they think they are. You are a great people surrendered to Me, yet with many flaws. Surrender it all. All your thoughts, all your desires for then I give you the desires of My heart. They will be much better. Yes My children, I said that I would give you the desires of your heart, but do you not know yet when your will is in my will you want me to choose for you? Can you grasp that? ***"I choose the best things for I give good gifts, perfect gifts to My children.***" Preach on little ones, for time is drawing nigh. I will come back soon and gather My bride to Me. I speak on: "Love not the world neither the things of the world. For I give you a heavenly kingdom which shall not pass away. I have spoken."

8-3-12 "The Truth Is Coming Out"

Thus saith the Lord: "Let the truth come out. The time is now for My servants to hear the sound of My voice. Put it off no longer for I be in the renewing of your minds. ***Transformation*** is on its way of which you are a part. The troops are coming in. What do I mean? Marching to the beat of My drum no longer weary, for I will bring a refreshing soon. What is in the refreshing? An abundance of rain. Who on? My people who are heartsick and weary. When will that be? Now for out of the abundance of rain, comes the revival fires falling. Take courage My people. Rejoice, for I will never leave you or forsake you. It will be a refreshing like you never knew before. ***"Take no thought of how this will come about for I am gathering My people now for the final victory."*** Do you not know yet I am the King of Kings and Lord of Lords? I dwell in the thick darkness. I meet you there children. Think I do not see you when you mourn for your loved ones? It shall be well, for I have spoken and I am God.

Dwell not in the thick darkness any longer, for I bring you out to the light. Many battles you have been having are over and victory is yours. ***"The truth has prevailed and as you stood for truth, I have stood for you."*** Believe more and I will reveal more. When you come out of your afflictions, I will meet you with the oil of gladness and a spring of living waters shall flow over in your souls. Speak on for out of your darkness has come light and out of your sorrow has come gladness. Now publish My word."

8-7-2000 "The Waves Crash But Tell The Story"

(Note: Spiritual understanding must be applied here, as of course there will be a new heaven and a new earth one day.) The Lord speaks: "You're on the new earth right now child. What do I mean? You're walking in eternal life now. Everyone is looking for a literal instead of a spiritual meaning. The spiritual comes first. I **will** destroy this earth one day but when will it be? It is now. It's **being** destroyed in men's hearts and minds. How? By loving Me more than they love the world. Then the world means nothing to them anymore. ***"Eternity is going on right now. How mean I? There is no beginning and no ending with Me. I am Alpha and Omega the Beginning and the Ending. I am all and in all."*** The waves tell the story. They crash!! They can't break down the rock. Jesus Christ is the rock. What am I saying? Only believe. What am I saying? The gates of hell cannot prevail against the church. What's the church? You are the saints of the living God."

6-11-12 "The Wheel Continues To Come Down"

Thus saith the Lord: "In the beginning was Adam and Eve and they sinned by the woman eating the forbidden fruit. Was it an apple? Was it an orange? That doesn't matter it was of no never mind-a piece of fruit. Now look at the matter closely. What happened? Eve gave place to the serpent and she listened and ate. What for? She was deceived and had to make a choice. She chose evil. She wanted her own wisdom, her own devices and the devil told her it was good fruit. Was it? ***"No it was rotten corrupt fruit."*** Where did Adam come into the picture? He chose his wife because that was the only way to buy her back. From what? Satan's snare. He had to do it for he was smitten with Eve. She was his companion. Was he right? Yes and no. How? The proof was in the pudding. How? Her sweetness was ever before him. Why did he choose Eve and the fall of the human race? He was working on another plan, his own to try to figure out what to do. ***"He chose wrong too. Now you see mankind was in a vice caught between heaven and earth and earth was holding him in its grip. What do I mean? The devil plotted against Eve from the beginning and won. He plotted against Adam and he won but he lost."*** Redemption's plan came into the picture. He chose wrong, but because of the wrong, I entered the picture. Now you see that perfect redemption's plan did enter in? I gave them the ***promise of a Savior*** and all was made right again. Only now, man would have to die and not live forever. Where do you go from here? To the beginning once again do you go and that is thus saith the Lord. Gird on new truth which is old truth. ***"Seek and ye shall find. Knock and it shall be opened to you. Under the altar Ezekiel saw motors of faith operating."*** Search it out, there are many wheels. Each in its own rotation or operation. How is that? Each one of you in the kingdom ride that wheel. It is where you get on or get off that makes all the difference. What you mean? ***"Eternity waits for no one, least of all you."*** Each day I draw you closer, the wheels turn. How's that? In reverse or forward do they turn. A reverse you say? They can't turn in reverse unless you let them. Why? How does that come about? If I draw you closer, you either resist or you climb aboard. You see you are a part of a process, not part of elimination. Study further. **Ezekiel 1:15-16** "Now as I beheld the living creatures, behold one wheel upon the earth by the living creatures, with his four faces. The appearance of the wheels and their work was like unto the colour of a beryl; and they four had one likeness: and their appearance and their work was as it were a wheel in the middle of a wheel." Now what does that say? Gloom, doom, joy and prosperity. There you have it. They are all intermingled, intertwined. Some come down righteous. Some come down unrighteous. It's the seed again we are talking about. Righteous seed or unrighteous seed. Study further. What you see? **Romans 10:17** "So then faith cometh by hearing and hearing by the word of God." Stop there and just say *"without faith it is impossible to please God."* They know it. The people know it but falter. They try to work their own salvation out within themselves. They do not work it out with fear and trembling before Me. They are wrong. It won't work. *"They stand by faith."* What do I have you do now? Come closer My people and hear this message well. For I have you hear it and live. Get to the root of the problem; *unbelief.* Sever the ties that bind you and stop at nothing to get at, to truth. Now you understand My people? Get off the sidelines; believe Me for I am bringing you into deeper truth. Nothing complicated, just simpler and deeper that is all. It has always been. You just didn't understand it for you had to get into the place where you could hear from Me. *"It is all in the word. I never leave My word."* It is solid. It is true. I give the ones listening ears to hear. Ask Me to clean your ears out and I will. Now deliver My word My child, for I have spoken and that is thus saith the Lord. I love My people and I come on the scene to revive, refresh and restore. Get off the sidelines. People, prepare for a day comes ahead that you will never stand without Me. *"Yet, if you draw nigh and hear My voice now you shall live and I will strengthen you and you shall live and prosper."* Now publish My word this time because, as long as you keep seeking, I keep adding and many get tired of the reading. Yet, I have chosen My elect that delights in My word and never tires of the sound of

My voice, speaking through this mouthpiece this day. Go in peace and I will receive you, guide you and anoint you with My love from on high. I speak. Hear Me well and that is thus saith the Lord. Get on fire, stay on fire and be refreshed this day for I am a kind and merciful God."

12- 21-12 "The Wings Were Talking And The Wheel Is Still Coming Down."

Ezekiel 10:1 "Then I looked, and, behold, in the firmament that was above the head of the cherubims there appeared over them as it were a sapphire stone, as the appearance of the likeness of a throne.

2 and he spake unto the man clothed with linen, and said, go in between the wheels, even under the cherub, and fill thine hand with coals of fire from between the cherubims, and scatter them over the city. And he went in in my sight.

3 now the cherubims stood on the right side of the house, when the man went in; and the cloud filled the inner court.

4 then the glory of the lord went up from the cherub, and stood over the threshold of the house; and the house was filled with the cloud, and the court was full of the brightness of the Lord's glory.

5 and the sound of the cherubims' wings was heard even to the outer court, as the voice of the Almighty God when he speaketh.

6 and it came to pass, that when he had commanded the man clothed with linen, saying, take fire from between the wheels, from between the cherubims; then he went in, and stood beside the wheels.

7 and one cherub stretched forth his hand from between the cherubims unto the fire that was between the cherubims, and took thereof, and put it into the hands of him that was clothed with linen: who took it, and went out.

8 and there appeared in the cherubims the form of a man's hand under their wings.

9 and when I looked, behold the four wheels by the cherubims, one wheel by one cherub, and another wheel by another cherub: and the appearance of the wheels was as the colour of a beryl stone.

10 and as for their appearances, they four had one likeness, as if a wheel had been in the midst of a wheel.

11 When they went, they went upon their four sides; they turned not as they went, but to the place whither the head looked they followed it; they turned not as they went.

12 and their whole body, and their backs, and their hands, and their wings, and the wheels, were full of eyes round about, even the wheels that they four had.

13 As for the wheels, it was cried unto them in my hearing, O wheel.

14 and every one had four faces: the first face was the face of a cherub, and the second face was the face of a man, and the third the face of a lion, and the fourth the face of an eagle.

15 and the cherubims were lifted up. This is the living creature that I saw by the river of Chebar.

16 and when the cherubims went, the wheels went by them: and when the cherubims lifted up their wings to mount up from the earth, the same wheels also turned not from beside them.

17 when they stood, these stood; and when they were lifted up, these lifted up themselves also: for the spirit of the living creature was in them.

18 then the glory of the Lord departed from off the threshold of the house, and stood over the cherubims.

19 and the cherubims lifted up their wings, and mounted up from the earth in my sight: when they went out, the wheels also were beside them, and every one stood at the door of the east gate of the lord's house; and the glory of the God of Israel was over them above.

20 This is the living creature that I saw under the God of Israel by the river of Chebar; and I knew that they were the cherubims.

21 Every one had four faces apiece, and every one four wings; and the likeness of the hands of a man was under their wings.

22 and the likeness of their faces was the same faces which I saw by the river of Chebar, their appearances and themselves: they went every one straight forward.

The Lord speaks about **Ezekiel 10:5**: "The wings were talking and they were crying out for mercy in the courts of the Lord." Why? They had no rest day or night. Why? The east wind was calling them. What does that mean you may ask? I will surely reveal. End time is coming and people better prepare. For what? Entering into the presence of the Lord like never before I surely say. What is this all about? Truth and righteousness are in the courts of the Lord. *East winds* are vehement are they not? Fierce strong winds that blow that about can knock a body down at times. *"My cherubims stand on the line and pronounce."* What, are they pronouncing, judgement? No crying out mercy, mercy, mercy. Read the whole chapter. Much will be revealed later on, but first for the learned, I have you examine the fifth verse. The truth is coming out and being revealed for those who want truth. Anyone in truth and in spirit seeks My face constantly. If you are not you are sliding back, I say unto you. Catch a new vision for a new day is surely upon you. Best to seek My face while I may be found, for surely some are being put on a shelf as I told you before through this vessel. My end time army is marching. Will you go forward or draw back? No place to run I say unto you. You have rested now get back into the battle, I say unto many of you. The evil one, the devil has a plan and he already has it mapped out for you. Heed him not for he would have you to stay on the sidelines and fight and you cannot do it that way. March forward, only proceed with caution, as the devil will try to catch you with *pride* and have you marching with a haughty step. I'll have it not. The wheel continues to come down, does it not? Is it a wheel of faith? Surely it is and many of you are riding the wheel down. *"The fifth wheel is in operation and I will reveal. It is the operation of grace I say unto the learned."* Four wheels have been in operation, now the fifth will begin. When you seek My face daughter, seek all of Me. You will not stop at your own explanations as you have none. You are just as baffled as many of the people as I reveal. I always take My little ones into further truth. Line upon line, precept upon precept. Catch the burden, the weight of what I am saying, My people.

"Five represents grace, does it not? Ride the wheel till the end

my children. Fifth wheel is symbolic I speak unto you. Get not off the wheel of grace and mercy. Faith till the end which will never end as that is the beginning." Ahhh... Now I got you... We are speaking about eternity are we not? I Am that I Am has sent you. Believe it not for surely I have spoken? *"A wheel within a wheel."* Much more will be added. Wait on me daughter. Some of the people are seeking to go further to understand My mysteries. Get in the flow I have spoken and a great God I am. I smile down upon you for your God sees your heavy burdens, your yokes. Yet remember My words unto you My children, My little ones, to come unto Me for my yoke is easy and My burden is light. Be refreshed this day My children, My little ones."

11-1-13 "Thirty Pieces Of Silver"

Heard the Lord speaking: "Judas Iscariot betrayed the son of man for thirty pieces of silver. What will My people betray Me for is the question the Spirit of the Lord doth ask? Know you not the sound of My voice My children? How I long to comfort you and be your all and in all? Get on the firing line and be done with it. The firing line is for all God's children. You must go through attacks, spiritual and otherwise, I do speak. *"Yet surely do many bring things on their own selves."* Avoid the question daughter? I will speak and will ask it. How do you that so long for Me in your hearts not finish the task I require of you? I speak now and not later for some of you. *"Obedience is the step that is required of you."* Gird on new strength for the journey. Bind up the wounds of many surely, but first hear the sound of My voice and live My people. *"You must regain ground and that can only be done by obedience. Hearken to the sound of My voice."* Why is your heart hurting? You left Me, the King of glory behind. Many of you and went your own way. You drifted too far from the shore little ones. *"Now come back all the way and I will fully receive you with open arms and then restore what the enemy has stolen."* Do you want no part of Me, My daughters and My sons? You have to receive it all, every bit of it. The correction is My chastening rod. Also love, kindness and compassion are My very nature. Know ye not there is a meek side of Me, gentle as a lamb? Yet there is also the roar of the lion. I am come that you may have life and have it more abundantly. I am that I am and surely do I speak soft words. Yet I also use the chastening rod at times. Which do ye prefer My children? Softly and tenderly do I call you. Obey Me and live. Who is this to? Whosoever will who needs it this day.

Don't look around My beloved children, for a loving father often brings correction and chastisement where needed. ***"If the shoe fits then wear it. If not, don't attempt to put it on."*** Warn my people, My daughter, for their blood will surely be on your hands if thou doest it not. A watchman on the wall you are and I will have mercy on those that repent and come back to Me in the fullness. For those that need no repentance, march on boldly for My name sake. Love you, I do every one and that is thus saith the Lord thy God this day.

"Time Is At Hand-Move Forward My Child"
Dream I had on 6-6-13:

I had walked back into a Baptist Church I used to attend for many a year. In this church, I had gotten saved as a child, and the Lord established some solid roots and foundation of the gospel in my life. Almost from a baby to 30 years old, I attended there. As I barely started walking down the aisle, the power of God was so very strong that I could not even 'stand' in the dream. I fell not only to my knees, but hit the carpet. There is 'no way' I can describe the 'glory of God' I felt. It was like it went beyond my dream state, and I was also in that 'glory dimension' in reality of the here and now! One thing I was pondering was the '<u>date</u>' I had the dream or more like a vision. The two numbers 6 and 13 stuck out. I inquired of the Lord and He asked me this question? "Did you not know that in the darkest hour I can visit?" We are going to experience a lot of shaking in these last hours, but God is going to show Himself powerful and faithful to see us through.

He keeps speaking to me about a **remnant** people. Heard the Lord speak about this dream, and knew it was to share with others after He released: "The power of God fell and the impact was higher and greater in the spirit than you had ever known or experienced. Glory in the extreme. Majesty, He reigns and let all God's people say amen, you tell the people. What has happened? *Transition-you are being taken into in this time of sorrow and affliction into a beautiful day of great victory and freedom.* That is what you are experiencing child, daughter. From a painful era you can hardly bear, stand to great light and magnitude to enter in. You can only hit the floor praising and magnifying Me. Glory, glory has come upon all My children walking in the glory world. Just step into this new season and be done with it. Winter season is done away; even spring season will soon be past. Summer the fullness is being realized. Let it all go; the past and move on, for I say on: many things that should have been in many hearts and lives were hindered, stopped by many factors. My people are hurting and I say on: great financial difficulties, relationships divided, afflictions of many kinds will be healed in this new day. Keep pressing on and in, for the great revival of the ages is upon you. My people are feeling the touches of it, but the greater glory of it has not even fallen yet. Many of your hearts have been wounded, stabbed by the very closest of associates, friends and neighbors. Pay it no mind, for what the enemy sought for evil, I only have it come out for good, if you only seek My face and turn not aside. Take steps forward never steps backward. Proof is in the pudding and I do get sweeter every day I do say unto your hearts little ones. There is a place in Me I am taking you to in this age; only yield, My children, My daughters and My beloved sons. Move out in the greater glory and let all shackles fall off you. Arise for the glory light does shine upon many of your faces. Others must repent of their evil deeds to partake of My glory in this end time army. Just be aware and mark those that do cause division and strife my children. Separate from them and pray they seek Me.

Let nothing or no one separate you from My great love, for you have seen nothing yet as you will if only you obey My voice and that is thus saith the Lord your God this day."

{Note: I know **'nothing'** can separate us from the 'love of God', but I also know that if we get off focus, and listen to man, instead of God, we are not walking upright then.

He is still loving us, that never changes! We then get out of step and are not realizing it then. Feel to explain, it is the 'flow', the communion here, I believe the Lord was speaking of.}

8-10-13 "Time Is At Hand, Quit Playing"

"Wreckage, carnage everywhere. I do speak to your heart. What am I speaking to you about child, daughter? Get the word out. Worry not what others think of you or are speaking, saying behind your back. For I do say unto your heart, the false prophets they do hear well. Chosen one of My remnant, I do speak and flow through you as well as many others all across the land. I have always had a people that did hear and obey the sound of My voice. Some even now are hungry and searching after Me. It is a late time and you all need to lay down everything on My altar of sacrifice. Get quiet, get alone with Me. The trouble is coming across this great land and is already here for those of you that have ears to hear. Many of you are stalling, lagging behind, for you are hearing the sound of the voice in the enemy's camp. Move out and forward My daughters and My sons, for much is being done behind your back, even now you know not of in this once great land. *"Be kind to one another My children; show the fruits of the spirit for they are needed greatly in this day and age."* My people are wounded greatly on the inside and many times you can only see the surface. Dig deep to help a person, My chosen ones, My leaders, but when I say pull back, then certainly do so, for I surely know the heart of all people. Leaders *lead* pure and simple I do say unto you. Get off the fence and get serious My people. Wake up, wake up, wake up. *"Time is at hand to hear My voice and stand and not fall down anymore."* I will see you through all things My children, My anointed ones, but all on the altar you must lay I speak again. Obey Me quickly and I will be your constant and surely be with you till the end. I am coming back for My children, My bride who have made themselves ready by the blood of the Lamb. Know My voice, obey Me and live and that is thus saith the Lord thy God. Sweetness is in My makeup. You who have only seen Me as a hard God, you have missed it entirely. I am surely *"sweeter than the honeycomb"* and love you I do. Feed My sheep, My lambs for they are hungry. I have spoken."

10-1-13 "Time To Get Still And Seek His Face"

Heard the Lord speaking: "Be alive in My presence, My children. Bask in Me. Come before My presence with singing. A new day is upon you. Let not your right hand know what your left hand doeth. Rejoice forevermore, for have I not said in My word that I would never leave or forsake you? Believe not My report little ones? Many of you are sick, wounded and your spirit is crying out for a release. I will never fail you my little ones, for I know not how to fail as mankind does. Get in the secret place, the coveted spot, for I will surely meet you there and we shall have sweet communion together. Do you desire to make it through the last days with victory in your souls? Then you must obey My voice. You will live and you will prosper as you seek My will, My approval in all things. *"Go not with the crowds, for they shall surely lead you wrong. It is not or has ever been about popular opinion."* Greet the dawning of each new day with praise on your very lips. Did you not know that I see your hearts, My beloved and desire to fill your cups to overflowing? Surely I will as you search for Me and long for Me with all your being. All you must lay on the altar of sacrifice. I never turn those away who worship Me in truth and in spirit, for all that come to Me must approach the throne in sincerity of everything that lieth within them. I say on: I inhabit the praises of My people. Only delight in Me and I shall bring things to pass shortly that you have been longing for. I encourage, I lift up My body this day. For I have seen the beating you have taken, many of you as of late. Turn the tables on the enemy. *"Stand fast."* Your defense is in

Me and I will surely move in your behalf, as you cry out to Me holy, holy, holy and yield to My biddings. I see when you surrender all, but also I see when many of My beloved ones and children draw back. No more! Come closer, for I will even tell you a secret in your ear and share many things. The closet is symbolic, but can be a literal place also. ***"Wherever you can go in and shut the door and be alone with Me, that is your private closet."*** I close with My love for you. Do you think your Heavenly Father doth not love you? Again I say, bask in My presence. Seek Me out. Delight in Me and walk in truth and ye shall prosper and that is thus saith the Lord your God this day."

11-3-12 "Trouble In The Land; Get Closer Unto Me"

I hear the Lord speaking: "Another day has dawned and still you are not any closer unto Me many of you. What is your problem? Did I not do enough My children when I gave My all on Calvary? Do you not know yet I love you, every one and no sacrifice was too great to pay for you? Why will you not give Me your all? You think the great God of glory cannot feel pain? Think again. Many think they are walking the walk and talking the talk, but yet I say on. Some may be, but many of you are not. This is to whosoever needs this. Chances are, if you think it is not for you, then it is for you. See I speak clear words of understanding. My children, who are walking in clear truth, hear My voice and examine their hearts every time. This is a tight walk and two can't walk it together I say. I walk beside you and it often is a lonely walk, but I see you through all things. Check your hearts for this be to all. If I never gave you warnings, then you would get heady and high-minded. Even if you are walking in the fullness, it is by My mercy and you need to realize this. Never get above your raising My children. What do I mean? When you are a little child, there is humbleness and there is a desire to see the beauty and simplicity in things. Next you grow up and I would have you always remember if you had humble beginnings. Even if you were privileged to be born into royalty, you should remember the poor. *"Don't get above yourselves is what I am talking about."* That is what I am coming to is instructions unto your hearts. Did you not know instructions should be a way of life? I speak again of what is coming on the land. *"Trouble, trouble, trouble and much pain and sorrow like you have never known before."* Why do you think I write this word so sharp? Think this sister desires to print it? No and yes. She would rather give an encouraging word, but she knows it is for your benefit. She is examining her own heart even as she types, as I have each one of you to do. The instructions are simple. Quit thinking, every one of you that you know anything. I give wisdom and knowledge and when you committed your soul unto Me, it was a precious thing. Think I do not desire to take you further? To make it through these troubled days you need full armor on. Many of you have full armor on but satan would desire to find a chink in it. You need to fully lean on My breast, as the Apostle John did at My last supper and hear My very heartbeat. Every one of you can get closer all the time and now is a new day. You need **a *fresh anointing*** and I long to pour it out on you. Yet I speak on: Why did John, Peter and the rest deny Me as I was taken before man before My crucifixion? You want to know? Fear entered in. That's right and fear will overwhelm you, unless you tighten your ships. This is to all and I say all. Scrunch up to Me, My children. Adore My face and live abundantly. You see the destruction that is coming on the land and even the world. It is bringing you into a new place in Me. *"It is a glory walk, the likes of which you have never known if you fully yield and pay the cost."* Fire *purifies* and you shall come through like gold. Walk on unafraid. How you say? As I say above, tighten your ships, love Me and seek My face. Everything is important to seek Me in. I have you walking unafraid in the midst of the storm. In fact you, My chosen ones, shall be helping and guiding many in these last days. I am raising up an army in these last days with absolutely *no fear*. Get ready. Fare ye well."

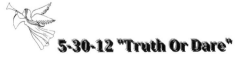

5-30-12 "Truth Or Dare"

Thus saith the Lord: "I speak truth. The world speaks lies. I reveal this day and not another to My people who have ears to hear truth. The wonder of it all is that I would abundantly pardon time after time again, but yet I do. *"How does error come in? When truth goes out the door there is room for nothing else but error."* Don't you see My children so many times you love a lie? *It is deep.* Get it all. Let Me in. Let Me in to your inward parts and I will reveal this day. *"Cain slew able and thus it begun."* Ah... But you thought it began with Adam and Eve. It did but it didn't. What do I mean? I will reveal. <u>John 1:1</u> <u>"In the beginning was the word, and the word was with God, and the word was God."</u> The enemy slips through when you not yield to Me in the fullness. We will come back to Cain and Abel. Begin. Look at the matters at hand. *"People buy a lie. How? By rejecting Me. There is room in your heart for only truth or error not both."* What I reveal in My word, it will carry you through and it is a solid word you can take to the bank. How does deception creep in? There are spirits in this world, as you all well know. They fell into place when Cain slew Abel. What I am talking about in this aspect only, is spirits started operating that day. Before then, when Adam and Eve fell, they still had the choice of righteousness, to partake of the tree of life. What was that about? Eternity and being bought back by the blood of the Lamb. Now begin your journey. Time and again you all have wondered what is or was going on in this world. So much confusion, chaos and trouble in the land. It entered through Cain's rebellion as far as wicked spirits entering the land. Sure Adam's fall brought in sin, sorrow and death, but look further My children. Take this moment and turn to: <u>1 John 5:6</u> <u>"This is He that came by water and blood, even Jesus Christ; not by water only, but by water and blood. And it is the Spirit that beareth witness, because the Spirit is truth."</u> What do you see here? Redemption's plan all over again. *"You see here children, the will has to be broken."* To some this is going, they need to see this great truth. They think it has but it hasn't and that is thus saith the Lord. Now put it together, the words I speak child. The water and the blood what is it? Redemption's plan all over again. I poured out life to you that day on the cross. *"My death brought life when I hung on that tree of shame and agony."* Don't you see My child, My children, the love the sacrifice that I paid that day when I hung there for your sins? Now begin again and bring them to Cain that slew Abel. Never was I so hurt and wounded as when man took another man's life. I cried just as you are crying now child as you write. I hurt plain and simple for I am a God of great compassion and I heard and felt *righteous Abel* cry out to Me. What was it about truly? Jealousy? Envy? Truly I say, but more than that. *It was about evil that had crept in Cain's heart;* pure and simple. Before now the heart of man was kept by Me and wicked spirits was not in him. My creation Adam and Eve had fallen, but truly they turned to redemption's plan and it was counted unto them for righteousness. They believed My report that the Savior would come and redeem them from sin. So they were covered by My blood for their faith. *"Now you see children? Cain entered in through unbelief."* Because he did not believe My report of a promised Savior then *deception* entered. Therefore the wicked spirits were allowed access. *"It was those spirits crying out in him to kill his brother Abel."* They are still crying out today. Get them out I say. How? *Hear truth only.* Don't want a lie? Then repent and be pure and stay pure in My sight. *"Obey Me children, for it is in disobedience every time the enemy steps in."* When you yield to Me, great peace comes in. When you falter and step back the enemy has gained ground as you gave him rights to proceed with his plan. Which is? Witchcraft spirits to take you over or whoredom spirits to gain access and control. Now which you want? *You want truth or a lie?* You got truth here between your eyes.

Believe my report and live and that is thus saith the Lord."

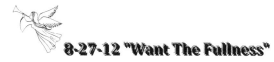

8-27-12 "Want The Fullness"

Thus saith the Lord: "As in times past, I call out to you again. Troubled are many of you and I give you the solution, if ye only listen. Why do you not come closer when I call you? Ye are blinded in part My children and I desire to take the blinders off. When will you learn of Me and My ways? I am dealing with your heart to come into the fullness and ye come not. Know ye not, I am a merciful Heavenly Father and with all you are going through, I long to succor you? I alone have the answers. Look unto Me and not to man children. Got problems? Yes you have many and the trials are getting worse and yet will they. Why would that be? Satan is loosed upon the earth and is running to and fro seeking whom he may devour. I'll have you quit trying to figure it out, for you can't. In this day and age it is a time of despair like never before. It is a day of trouble and a cloudy day. *"Visit the throne room and then you will know. What do you mean? You are not as close as you think you are. Children, the closer you come unto Me, the more you see you are not as close as you think you are."* Jump in the waters. I have rivers of living water flowing out of your bellies. What would that be about? When you get so full you can't help to flow out to others. It will be gushing out of you and you won't be able or desire to stop it. You can't plug up an overflow of this size, My children. When you get in the overflow, nothing will compare unto it. Love Me, serve Me and know that Holy Ghost fire is being poured out across the land. Seek Me like never before and I will pour out My Spirit upon you. Know you not the Holy Ghost should be poured out unto you without measure? You, my children are going to need to be in the fullness as never before. March on to victory. Come unto the rivers of living waters and live."

8-24-12 "What About The Mark?"

Thus saith the Lord: "Know ye not the mark is fast approaching my children? It is even here now, open your eyes. What would it be? 666 is a number, the number of a man right? I explain further. Take My number My children and you will never take the mark of the beast. What would My number be? You should know this by now, but I will reveal. It is 777. Many of you have it stamped upon your foreheads already, some do not. What am I talking about? Coming unto Me and getting in the fullness is whereof I speak. Know you not you can get so deep in Me you will never desire to turn back? I speak unto ye My children, to quit worrying about the mark and make sure you have Mine embedded in your forehead and or hand. The world has been deceived with the rapture theory. The great tribulation is right now not out there somewhere, where you will be mysteriously air lifted up out of all trouble. The church world has it backwards, I speak unto you. Hear the sound of My voice and live. You are entering a time of trouble like never before, but I will keep you through it. I will not rapture My people out of trouble, but give you great joy in the midst. Quit fiddling around and wake up I say. The wicked are going to get more wicked and the righteous are going to shine forth brighter in the gross darkness coming on the land. You say later, I say now. There is a robe of righteousness I have My children wear. Am I talking about in heaven? Wake up My people, I am creating a new heaven and a new earth when you are ready. Wake up I say again. Come alive in Me and take on the fullness or ye shall not be able to withstand My children. I am visiting many with My chastening hand yet with much love and tender mercies. The mark cannot even be a temptation to the ones who have sold out to Me lock, stock and barrel as the world says. I have you, give it all. Lay everything down at my feet. Children you are trying to give Me part of you. Give your whole selves. Live, cry out and breathe only Me. Then, when you are in that place, the transformation that takes place will amaze you. Are you wholly

Mine or part Mine? Wake up I say again. It is not too late yet, but I say get locked into your choice of the fullness or go backwards. I don't want your jewelry or a clothesline religion; I just want you My children. Quit trying to figure it out. I say again I want you. When you are consumed wholly on my altar of sacrifice, then you will gladly lay down anything that is hindering your growth. Fare ye well. Look ye not at the storm clouds brewing across the land. What do I mean? Yes, I have you to be aware of the times and to get your head out of the sand, but I want to visit you in a more perfect way. Lay it all down and the heights I take you to will be indescribable. Let every beat of your heart feel My embrace, My touch and My love. Hear the sounds of the universe again I tell you. I say again, hear the earth travailing and giving birth. It is a new day dawning and all creation is crying out for the fullness. Be a part. The rocks still cry out when men don't praise me. Snuggle up to Me, My children for I long to comfort you and give you joy everlasting. ***It is I that will see you through these great and terrible days***. Fare ye well and love you I do."

2-21-13 "Which Camp Shall It Be?"

Hearing the Lord speak: "As it was in the days of Noah, so shall it be in the days of the coming of the son of man. Great tribulation and stress to the nations is upon you and you see it not, My daughters and My sons I say unto you. You see in part, many of you and feel things will continue on as before. I say **not so.** For surely I the Lord do speak unto your hearts, to consecrate yourselves continually unto Me for these coming days. Satan desires to sift you as wheat and many of you shall fall by the wayside, if you do not get rooted and grounded deeply in Me. I say surely the battle is on and your warfare is being taken to a new level in these last days. My people, with the stronger fight comes the greater victory. ***"Fasting time is upon you my beloved, to hear clearer from Me and to break the yokes off others. It is in My word, read it."*** Many are seeking to come into an easier door, there is none. Some are still fighting battles of the heart with ones I have surely not put with you. Why My daughters and My sons are ye not heeding the voice of your God, patiently warning you time and again? It is because there is deception and it has pulled the wool over your eyes My beloved, My children. You will be rended by their spirits operating and taken down a long and wrong road. Have it not, but return unto Me in the fullness and I will fix your hearts, My little ones. For surely I do speak again through this sister as before time, that two can never walk together unless they have agreed. Make your decision, for I say unto you it is *time and past* when you should have broken away. Buy not their evil report. They speak lies dipped in deception and try to capture your heart with their web spun. We go back to the beginning which is also the ending. For yeah I say on: you are blinded in part and many have let the world put the blinders over your eyes about many things. Come out of her, My people and be not partakers of her sinful ways, that ye receive not of her plagues. They are surely being poured out even now as we speak. Control, government control is what is going on. Open your eyes for you think you see clearly, but many of you do not even know, I say unto you. Repentance is what is needed for this nation. Will they do it? I say unto you yes and no and will explain. A small majority, a *remnant*, have always pulled away from the world and heard My voice clearly. The rest just march to the beat of their own drum and the worlds. Chaos and confusion is in the land and much deception. Cry out My people, My beloved ones, for I am hearing a sweet sound from heaven when you do. It is surely music in the sound of Mine ears. I love you My people and delight not in allowing destruction to come on the land, but surely it must. *"With your cries that come before Me, many will be spared in the land."* There is strength in numbers. Only closely associate with others of great focus and love of the gospel. Love all, but come not in close alliance with anyone unless you are going down the same pathway together. I will have a church washed clean by the blood of the Lamb, spotless white. I am getting her ready, My bride for My second coming. No compromise will be in her, a people *running* to do My blessed will. Obedience is in their hearts and they delight in Me only. There are two camps and I will reveal further. ***"It is surely a world system that I am speaking of and warning you, My children, My beloved ones. It is an 'enemy's camp' that I have you not a part of. It is of Baal worship plain and simple."*** It has always been, but there is a true and a living God with true prophets who will not prophesy a lie to your hearts. They tickle not your ears. Hear them well, but know the difference, for there is much false in the land. The 'saint's camp' I would surely have you walk in. Quit switching camps, some of you, for do you not know yet that sweet and bitter water plainly will not mix? I have spoken. Take My words here and try the spirits. I am straightening up my church, those who will listen and be corrected. My chastening rod is upon some of you. I only rebuke and chasten those I love. Did you not know about the potter's wheel? Stay on it and be fashioned in My glorious likeness. Love you I do My people. Walk in My footsteps and establish your ways only in righteousness. Let all the earth rejoice and bow down and worship Me only. It is all about the heart condition. Get it right and that is thus saith the Lord your God."

"Word of the Lord for 2013"

"Depth persuasion- I am bringing many into this deeper walk with me. Commitment, it is all about commitment. As you walk and talk with Me and delve into Me, deeper and deeper will you go. Many chains shall fall off in 2013 that heretofore has bound you. I, your God have seen your pain and set out to heal you. Discover not another, for I will be your first love and I will be your last. The key to victory is praise. Praise on, rejoice on, for it is I thy God that healeth thee. Take new steps in 2013 that I have ordained. I will open doors. I will show you also that many doors have been closed. What I have set out before you prophets of God, is for you to prophecy like never before. Many of you shall speak to the nations of My great goodness in this new year before you. I shall use all in My kingdom who will let. From the least to the greatest is needed. I say again all members in My body are needed. I persuade you, I draw you daughters and sons to come alive in 2013. I am not a dead God. I visit. I say again come alive in 2013. I am persuading you, I am calling you. Victory is mine saith the Lord and I will repay for your obedience. I see it all, to the faithful I do speak. Now, rest in My word and watch Me perform it and that is thus saith the Lord."

"Word of the Lord for 2014"

"Enemy lines are drawn. Prepare My people for truth or dare. Which side of the fence are you on? I send you an encouraging word, but first the admonishment. Get on fire and quit worrying about the past. Know you not the future is in My hands and there is nothing you can do of what is behind you? All I say truly you must do is learn from your mistakes. *"Let it go; let it all go, but moving into the things of your God for this coming year. 2014 is a year of 'accomplishment' for many."* You will get where you have never been if you will wrap yourself in Me and keep your focus, your eyes on Me only. I will take you higher and exalt you. People many times will distract you and destroy your focus from Me. Let it not, allow it not. *"New grounds you are gaining if you listen to the sound of My voice."* I am taking you places you have never been in the coming year, I speak again. New commitment, new fire and new zeal; for My anointing is surely upon you. I speak a good word, a kind word and encourage My people this day. Read the word. All on the altar you must lay My people. Approved unto Me and My service, for vain is the works of many. Know ye not that I am protecting you even guiding you with My eye? Instruction is in my courts. Take heed to your ways little ones for I long to take you higher. *"Examine your hearts and move in My flow for this coming year."* What is it all about my children being taken higher by Me? Do you exalt yourselves? Of course not, but as you humble yourself, I am setting you on high and using you in My kingdom. I cannot use haughtiness in a person, pride. Make your boast in the Lord your God alone. All else will fail, fall and crumble. Sweetness is in My nature and I surely love you. Do you want to follow Me? Then know the cost is great, but the benefits are many. For the ones who shut their selves up with Me, there is great reward. *"Know the secret place, the intimate place of worship with Me."* Come apart for a while to draw closer and I will stamp My mark of beauty upon you. Did you not know My children when you draw nigh to Me that others see Me in you? You are truly lights unto the world. *"Then ye shall see many chains fall off in the coming year and true freedom you shall walk in. I will take you places you cannot even imagine in the spiritual realm and even in the natural realm. I have decreed it."* Now wait on Me for more daughter, for I am concluding the matter. What is it all about? The enemy tries to deceive, but it is so simple even a child can understand. *In Me there is true freedom.* Discourse for action. What do I mean? *"Let all things go behind you; I speak again and move forward, taking no steps back. Quit straddling the fence and believe I have called you for such a time as this My children.* "Then you will prosper like never before in your soul for this coming year. I will use you and cause many of you to work in even *new fields of opportunity* and that is thus saith the Lord your God this day."

"Word of the Lord for 2015"

"Peace I speak unto your heart. I bring you into a deeper walk with Me if only you let. You are in a decision making process for the new year. Make up your minds many of you, which way you will go, for I am looking for the faithful. The ones who hear My voice well and obey Me. You want a word; you shall get it, an awesome word of responsibility and direction, My people. Take no steps backward, only forward in this new year of covenant with Me. Learn to let the past go, My daughters and My sons, for a higher rung (*Def.'step of a ladder'*) ; you shall climb on the ladder of success. In my kingdom all things matter and have begun. To succeed in *righteousness* begin and end in Me. Let My thoughts consume you be filled with My presence. ***Holy is My name.*** Doors shall open, doors shall close in this coming year. I will take you where you have never been. People need your help and your faltering days are over and done away with. Joy and laughter will come upon you and you shall sing a ***new song.*** Blinders will come off and ye shall see clearly which way to go and the direction to take. Go back to the beginning, the cornfields and get the basics. ***"I am taking you higher, but you have to get lower to get there."*** Learn of Me, for I am truly setting you apart for this new year and you are coming out and going over the top."

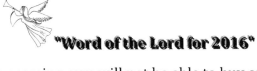

"Word of the Lord for 2016"

"There is a day coming, you will not be able to buy or sell. Prepare now. Come closer unto Me. Repair the breach. Move on forward. Let the past go My children, My beloved ones. Altar, lay it all down. 2016 is a year of 'new awakening'. Guided missiles on the launch pad are you. Branch out in new directions. Know ye not the sound of My voice? Go where I lead you. Next season is a hard one, but a blessed one. Many shall rise up against you, but know My voice. I shall lead you out calling you to higher grounds. There is nothing hidden that shall not be revealed, uncovered. Go forward, watch, prepare and guide My people. Be alert. Humble thyself in My sight and I shall lift you up. I have spoken."

8-12-12 "Wrath Has Fallen"

Thus saith the Lord: "The tidal wave has come. The floodgates of My power are being unleashed. I am coming on the scene and pouring out My fury on the nations for their disobedience. I am having mercy on who will let. Many of My people will come back to Me, their God, as separated they have been. Never has there been a time to serve Me as now. Angels are guarding you, My children, for I have it to be so. Look out your windows, many will begin to see of which I speak. Are they visible? Yes and no. What do I mean? Many will see the light and many have already seen. You think not I love My people? Love you I do, yet many times I have pulled back My hand on blessing you. What is that is about? The truth must prevail. Error is in the camp. I tell you time and time again that I draw you closer. Why you not yield? Guide Me in truth you say, but yet you resist and pull back. I visit you this day. Make your minds up. Go with Me all the way or not? Your choice, but I desire to bless you as never before. Get out of the dark. Am I talking to the sinner? No I am talking to My children. You all are My children if only you yield to Me. A curse has struck the nation. They better repent or I destroy them all. Yet I fulfill my word in the book of **Malachi**. What I say in the **Third Chapter Fifth verse**? Look it up. A nation that heeds not My voice will not heed this, but yet My children of the remnant recognize and believe. My word says:

"And I will come near to you to judgment; and I will be a swift witness against the sorcerers, and against the adulterers, and against false swearers, and against those that oppress the hireling in his wages, the widow, and the fatherless, and that turn aside the stranger from his right, and fear not Me, saith the Lord of hosts."

Publish My word child. It speaks for itself and the people either believe it or not. Many things will be avoided if only the people will repent and cry out for mercy for the land. Come ye closer unto Me, the King of kings and Lord of lords. Spread My word, everywhere you go. It is a message of repentance and coming back to their first love. I have spoken. Love you I do, but falter not."

10-14-14 "Your Will, Your Way, or Mine"

What I heard the Spirit of the Lord speak: "You think many thoughts that bombard your mind with error many times, My children. Be approved of Me, footsteps in the sand. I walk with you. I talk with you. Recovery of the lean years, I say unto your heart, chosen ones. I am bringing a blast, a trumpet call for all who hear My voice. There is a remnant set forth for this hour. This is a remnant who will not bow down to any other God and serve them. Holy waters do they desire. People who know My voice and will not walk in error. Still they must examine their hearts, their motives, for the enemy would desire them to lose track. There is nothing hidden that shall not be revealed, little ones. You want truth, walk in it; the newness of life, ordained for this very hour. Holy manna from above, tempest tossed are many of you, but I am bringing you out. A higher calling and set apart to hear My voice only. Where will it be? In the church houses, out on the streets, in the midst of a multitude? Wherever you are, there am I in the midst of you. The written word, explore it. I am in it, the pages of My holy word. Still, which one shall you read with so many versions around? Man errs in his own opinions many times and adds or takes away from My word, daughter. They decide to write a ***different version*** and there you go. Each one is slanted in their own opinion and deceit, unless they are filled with the Holy Ghost and power from above. Everything that has breath must praise Me daughter. All on the altar you must lay it all. Come under subjection and live, period. Father of lights in whom there is no variableness of turning. ***"Any version without the power of God in it is dead."*** Believe My report. Are there many, are they few? Are they slanted toward one opinion or another? What is truth? What is fallacy? ***"The very foundation of the truth is based on the gospel of Jesus Christ period."*** Without Me there is no light in men. How did they go wrong? They heard it through the grapevine. Some wanted recognition and power of men. Others wanted control, wealth and fame. Still, there are the pure in heart who sought Me out on the beloved scriptures. Try My word see if it will stand? Is it pure, undefiled or slanted in man's opinions? Be careful My daughters, My sons, for it is the age of much deception. Rightly divide it for it will set you free. Throw the rule book away and live unencumbered from bread from above. My yoke is easy and My burden is light."

60077620R00074